ESSENTIAL

SCANDINAVIAN

STYLE

or before th
me

D1362974

0066722

66722

ESSENTIAL
SCANDINAVIAN
STYLE

ROSALIND BURDETT

WARD LOCK

A WARD LOCK BOOK

First published in the UK 1995
by Ward Lock
Wellington House
125 Strand
LONDON
WC2R0BB

A Cassell Imprint

First paperback edition 1998

Distributed in the United States
by Sterling Publishing Co., Inc.
387 Park Avenue South, New York,
NY 10016-8810

A British Library Cataloguing in
Publication Data block for this book
may be obtained from the British
Library

ISBN 0-7063-7748-6

Designed by Nick Clark
Illustrations by Jane Hughes
Printed and bound in Spain by
Bookprint S.L.
Front cover photograph:
Robert Harding Picture
Library/Chris Drake
Back cover photograph:
Courtesy of Hülsta

CONTENTS

$\mathcal{I}$NTRODUCTION

EXTREMES OF LANDSCAPE, TEMPERATURE AND LIGHT epitomize Scandinavia. The darkness of the long, harsh winters contrasts with the brightness and lush vivacity of the hot summers. Then there are the geographical extremes – the high, inaccessible mountains, the dense forests, the coastal areas and the meadowed, arable lands – which bring to Scandinavia a unique beauty. A land which obliges its inhabitants to live under such polarities creates an independent and community-minded people, with a strong sense of their own cultural individuality.

So, is there a specific Scandinavian style for interiors? To answer that, we need to look more closely at Scandinavia itself. It is made up of five widely different countries: Denmark, Finland, Iceland, Norway and Sweden. Within each of these countries, there is an enormous wealth of individual traditions and influences. It is thus an extremely rich heritage from which to draw inspiration for decorative styles; all the small influences have come together to create a wonderful array of characteristics. Small wonder, then, that the term 'Scandinavian style', today, can mean an enormous range of interior decoration.

For the purposes of this book, we can compress and adapt all this abundance into three fairly disparate styles. Having decided which look is the one for you, this book will help you to achieve that look in your own home, room by room, by analysing the elements that go to create it.

PEASANT FARMHOUSE STYLE

Most of the inspiration for this is drawn, as you may expect, from rural cottages dating from 300 to 400 years ago where the owners scratched a living, often from farming. The houses were rustic and sturdily built by the owners from logs or planks of local wood. Timber was enormously important to all Scandinavians, particularly those in the north, as Scandinavia is a very densely forested land. Wood was used for building houses, making furniture, and

*This bright peasant-style sitting
room, with its red-painted timber
walls and decorative cushions and
fabrics sings with pattern and colour.*

constructing all manner of other things, from farming tools to beautifully carved, purely decorative items.

Several generations of the family often had to live in the same house, so space was carefully utilized. Bedrooms were ingeniously conjured out of nowhere, and furniture often folded or had a dual purpose. This also created a reason and a method for extending the farmhouse; the son would add a new room for himself and his new wife.

The long dark winters meant that indoor crafts flourished. In addition to woodmaking and carving, there was also a superb tradition of tapestry and needlework from these northern countries. Each region tended to have its own patterns, which were worked as cushions, rugs, blankets or saddlebags. Many examples still exist in Scandinavian museums today, and the patterns are a rich source of folklore. Weaving was prevalent, particularly of narrow floor runners in wonderful bright colours.

But it is the exuberant painting on walls and furniture, both inside and out, which seems to be exclusively Scandinavian. There are hundreds of different forms of painting; there was Norwegian *rosmålning* (literally, rose painting, relying heavily on floral motifs) and Swedish *kurbitz* (specifically from the province of Dalarna) with its flamboyant and imaginative designs. Each country and even each village evolved their own colours and designs; the fresh colours were mixed by hand with natural ingredients and brightened the whole house.

GUSTAVIAN STYLE

The second form of decoration, designated Gustavian style, is based on a much more stylized and sophisticated form of interior design. Taking its name from King Gustav III of Sweden (1771–1792), under whose patronage the style developed, it was an amalgamation of the clean lines and restraint of classicism with the exuberance of rococo curves. It was inspired by European styles of furniture and architecture of the period, notably French and English, but Gustav's own craftsmen put a uniquely Nordic stamp on their work.

A Gustavian-inspired bedroom with characteristic high, light walls, polished wooden floors and pale-coloured furniture. The sage green provides a restful atmosphere for sleeping.

The characteristics of a Gustavian interior are sophisticated symmetry, pale colours and high, light rooms, enhanced by large windows, many mirrors and sparkling chandeliers. Walls, often hung with canvas, were painted with simulated panels, columns and other classical devices, enlivened by painted swags of foliage, posies, garlands and laurel wreaths. Floors were polished wooden boards, or parquet in the grander houses. Ceramic stoves had just been invented; the heat they produced enabled a room to be used in its entirety. The painted ceramic tiles on these stoves were often works of art in their own right.

Gustavian furniture was classically elegant in style, with restrained carved ornamentation, with perhaps a carving of a swag or a garland decoration on the back. The whole item was usually painted in pastel colours to blend with the rest of the room. The aristocracy obviously evolved this style but, around this time, Scandinavia began to manufacture items in factories, bringing furnishings into the reach of more ordinary households. Gustavian style therefore became very popular all over Scandinavia, and not just with the nobility.

The uncluttered interior, functional furniture and large-paned windows allowing in plenty of light are typical of up-to-the-minute contemporary decoration, Scandinavian style.

MODERNIST APPROACH

The third style does not hark back to tradition. It is the most contemporary, dating exclusively from the latter half of the 20th century. Finnish architect, Alvar Aalto, and Danish architect, Arne Jacobsen, among many others working around the post-war period, were exponents of this form of design. The style became synonymous with Scandinavia in the 1960s and 70s, as no other country was dealing with contemporary design in quite such a courageous way at this time.

The feeling of this style is one of spaciousness: the lines of interiors and furniture are clean-cut and uncluttered, decorations and patterns are unfussy and minimal. Light is maximized by big windows with large panes, and simple, if any, curtain treatments. White is a favourite colour, with well-designed functional furniture, either painted white, or beautifully made from blonde wood. Materials used are natural – woods, slub cottons and wool. Accessories are carefully chosen and arranged, and even flowers should have architectural merit to blend well, such as lilies, freesias, and so on.

So there are three quite different Scandinavian styles. For your own Scandinavian-style home, you will probably find you prefer one of these looks. Choosing a theme to follow throughout your home, and adhering to a set of principles like this, will lead to a sense of harmony in all the interiors. This will impart a stylish coherence to your home, creating a unified whole.

However, if you really have difficulty choosing which

Scandianvian style you like, you could perhaps combine different Scandinavian styles in different rooms. Or, with care, it is possible to blur the edges between the different styles. Take inspiration from Scandinavian experts. At the end of the last century, Swedish artist Carl Larsson's Arts and Crafts home in Sundborn, north of Stockholm, had (and still has) great influence on homes all over Scandinavia and the rest of the world – much as William Morris was setting that style in England. For his dining room, which shouts with contemporary colour and pattern, Carl Larsson commissioned Gustavian-style chairs which he painted to match his wife's bold textiles; the chairs in the living room, which they inherited, are also distinctly Gustavian in feel. With their frilled seat cushions in checked cotton, they look absolutely right.

In this way, you could have a single folk-painted item of furniture in an otherwise loosely Modernist room, or one modern pale wood cupboard with clean-cut lines in a mainly Gustavian room. But take care – too much combining of styles in one room is likely to create an uncomfortable and restless interior.

After first looking at the colours and fabrics you will need to create a Scandinavian-style decor, the following chapters offer advice on how you can create whichever Scandinavian look you like, in whichever room you like. Each chapter also includes projects, with easy-to-follow instructions.

A view from the dining room through to the living room in Carl and Karin Larsson's home in Sundborn. Note the easy mix of Gustavian and contemporary styles.

CHAPTER ONE

COLOURS, FABRICS AND TEXTURES

In this room are illustrated the elements of Nordic peasant-style interiors: colourful patterned fabric, with a stencilled appearance and painted wooden furniture.

THIS CHAPTER IDENTIFIES, IN A GENERAL WAY, those colours, fabrics and textures available today which help to create each of the three main Scandinavian styles. This book is not about how to achieve complete authenticity in a Scandinavian interior, rather how to identify the elements of the look that you like, and use these to create an interior that is right for you and your family.

Fortunately, for anyone interested in creating Scandinavian style in their homes today, the materials that were used 200, 300, or even 400 years ago are, for the most part, as readily available now as they were then. In some cases, present-day materials are even better than the original. Timber is still plentiful, but MDF (medium density fibreboard) is an excellent material for the mass production of furniture which will have a painted surface; it can even be moulded into Gustavian-type carvings and details. Paint, nowadays available ready mixed, can be bought in an enormous range of relevant colours. It can be easily diluted, or alternatively rubbed away from the backgound coating, to create a faded, aged effect.

WALLS

Walls in Scandinavian interiors should be cool and serene, reflecting the cold northern

In a white-on-white interior, the decorative interest comes from contrasting textures, which are here achieved by the play of different fabrics and woods.

light of the land. This holds true, generally, across all three of the Scandinavian styles.

The brightest colours would be found in folk cottages as the peasants sought to cheer the long winters but, to recreate the look now, these colours should be muted and faded, to mimic the passage of time. Folk-style patterns in paint can be created very quickly now with ready-cut stencils. There is also a variety of rustic patterned wallpaper available, ready for an instant peasant farmhouse look.

Restrained, almost severe, colour schemes of the whitest shades of pastel pale were the norm in the Gustavian era, and so they should be included in any replica of that period today. Wallpaper with a small all-over pattern in glaucous blues, greens or greys would be in keeping, although there is nothing stopping you having pink if you like it. The appearance of Gustavian-style painted panels is not too difficult to achieve yourself.

Contemporary Scandinavian style is very understated in colour, as it places more emphasis on the architectural shapes

Floorboards in polished blonde wood, showing an interesting woodgrain, are perfect for any Scandinavian-style interior.

involved than the shades. However, small injections of sharp colour serve to make a decorative statement; the contrast often brings the interior to life.

FLOORS

The most authentic Scandinavian flooring for any room in the house is that of stripped floorboards. Wide, rough-hewn boards are most in keeping with rustic interiors, while a beautifully finished wood, or even parquet, floor is right for the Gustavian style. Polished planks of well-matched wood with an interesting grain typify the minimalist look. Indigenous carpets were rare; rugs were more usual. The most authentic of these would be long narrow runners, usually made from woven cotton. Runners are available today from specialist shops but, for a rustic or summer house interior, it would be possible to join several similar woven rag rugs together.

TEXTURES AND FABRICS

One of the most important textures in Scandinavian interiors is, of course, timber. A piece of wood, polished lovingly so that the grain gleams, is a thing of great beauty, be it a floor, a piece of furniture or a small box. It can be polished to glossy smoothness, or be carved into weird and wonderful shapes.

But softer textures, provided by natural woven textiles, are pertinent too. Cotton and wool can be thick and slub-woven, or fine and patterned. Checked fabrics in soft colours are relevant to Scandinavian interiors, as are small all-over sprigged or floral fabrics.

Scandinavians are keen to let in as much light as possible to their interiors, so sheer fabrics for curtains are important. There is a wide variety available today, not just of net; and they can be used to create lovely ethereal effects when draped at windows.

FURNITURE

Wood is very important to Scandinavians, and it can be used to make any piece of furniture, in whatever style required. It can take an enormous variety of finishes – polished, painted or carved, or all three!

Rustic furniture has a friendly, hand-carved look, and there is a wealth of painted patterns to add to its character and charm. (Unfortunately, Scandinavian painted furniture is too large an area for this book to look at in detail.)

Original Gustavian furniture dates from the late 18th century. But this fashion is enjoying a great surge of popularity 200 years later. Many furniture manufacturers today are drawing inspiration from this period, taking the best elements of those and combining them into sleek new originals, which makes it a lot easier to create this style in your home!

Modern furniture is a matter of choice. You decide what look – and what budget – you want to go for. Investing in beautiful handmade contemporary furniture is definitely worth the money. These pieces are the antiques of the future and will become heirlooms for the generations to come.

Sheer fabric curtains, either white or pale-coloured, let light in beautifully, and are much favoured by Scandinavians.

CHAPTER TWO

HALLS

FIRST IMPRESSIONS ARE VITAL. The first view of anything, or anywhere, you see will colour your whole opinion of that object or place. The same obviously applies to a house, and it is the hall which is the first part of your home that visitors will see.

Because the hall is not usually a place where you spend a lot of time, it is easy to forget that this space is not just a link between the other rooms in a house. A hall should be considered as a room in its own right, and should be decorated in keeping with the rest of the house. And since the hall is where visitors enter your home, this is the room which will create the first impression of your entire house. If you have decided to choose a particular decorative theme or influence for your home, make sure your hall is part of that and does not jar with the rest of the house.

First and foremost, you want to create a welcoming atmosphere in the hall. A lived-in feel will make a hall seem inviting

1 *Pale-coloured walls, paintwork in honey tones*

2 *Natural flooring – seagrass – adds warmth*

3 *Cheerful checked curtains add a welcoming feel*

4 *Plenty of furniture gives a lived-in look*

5 *Decorative wooden rack painted with a dark colourwash over red*

6 *All kinds of Scandinavian details, including a willow wreath and carved clock, combine for a cosy look*

and friendly. So, find a tiny corner for a chair or table, and hang pictures on the walls. Add a bunch of flowers, and your hall immediately has colour and life, instead of the starkness and lack of purpose which is often evident in halls. Having ensured that you are making the best of your hall, and are utilizing all its space with imagination and efficiency, now is the time to think about Scandinavian-style decoration.

WALLS AND CEILINGS

Because the rooms that a hall links are arranged on the exterior walls with most of the access to windows, the hall itself sometimes lacks natural light. So, this is where one of the most simple of Scandinavian schemes – pale colours and blonde woods – is absolutely perfect. Pastel, even crisp white, walls maximize what little light there is and look coolly stylish, while ceilings in those colours will bounce reflected light back into the room. Colourwashing can be effective here, with its translucent layers of colour. It is also an easy paint effect to achieve (see page 25).

Halls have lots of doors to incorporate into the colour scheme, not to mention staircases, corridors and changes of level. If your hall is rather small, it is probably best to paint all the doors, door frames, bannisters, and so on, the same colour as the walls; the texture of gloss or eggshell against the matt emulsion will add an extra dimension. If you have a little more space to play with, it is still best to keep to similar tones, with the woodwork in a darker shade of the walls to add some, but not too much, definition; this will preserve the simple restrained Scandinavian look.

FLOORS

Stripped and polished wooden floorboards are the best floorcovering for any Scandinavian interior. The glow and living character of the planks look superb, and the hardwearing qualities are particularly relevant for a hall. You can stencil and/or colour timber so that it will blend with the exuberant look imparted by Nordic hand-painted furniture, or leave it bare for the austere

sophistication of Gustavian style. Planks are good, too, for the robust peasant look, as long as they are not too smooth or highly polished. Indeed, the floor should not really be polished at all in a hall, as that would create a slippery, highly dangerous surface, especially lethal on stairs.

One point that is pertinent for halls is that timber floors can be noisy underfoot, particularly when going up or down the stairs, so you may prefer to choose a natural floor covering such as coir or sisal; the natural tones of these coverings still look reasonably authentic. You could combine both options, having sanded floorboards on ground level, and carpet or matting on the stairs and upper landings.

WINDOWS
As windows in a hall are often small, and there is not much natural light, sheer fabrics or nets are a good Scandinavian-style option for

A pretty arrangement of Scandinavian-style folk crafts looks homely and welcoming in a corner of the hall.

Polished floorboards give a very Scandinavian appearance to a hall; you could add painted stencilled decoration for a folk-style look.

hall curtains. However, if you have ill-fitting windows which need the insulation of thicker curtains, checked cotton or a material with a natural slubby weave would look good. You could perhaps use brighter coloured curtains here than in the rest of the house, to add a sense of cheery welcome.

One way to maximize what natural light you can in a hall is to knock out the wooden upper panels in solid doors, and then replace them with glass. This will allow a lot more daylight in, and it looks good too.

LIGHTING

Obviously, for safety reasons, halls must be lit adequately, especially stairways; each tread must be clearly visible. Fixed fitments are best, either ceiling- or wall-hung lights. Lamps are not ideal because of trailing flexes though, if you have a built-in piece of furniture, a lamp can sit very nicely on that and cast an inviting pool of light. Wall-hung fittings illuminate more softly, throwing less harsh shadows than pendant ceiling lamps. If you have a really narrow corridor, making wall lights impractical, use directional spotlights or wallwashers which aim the light down the walls. These would work well anywhere in the hall.

FURNITURE

A lived-in, furnished feel gives a hall an inviting and relaxing atmosphere. So, if possible, tuck a piece of furniture somewhere in the hall. There is always room even in the tiniest hall for a little table, or at least a shelf, for a plant or vase of flowers. But, if you do have a bit more space, add a chair – Gustavian-style would be excellent – or, if possible, a sofa, along with a table or small chest nearby. This is just the place for the post, keys, messages, the telephone, and so on.

A hall is a good place to site a single piece of furniture that does not neccessarily go with other pieces, as it can stand on its own. You could refurbish a junk-shop find, sanding it down to give a new smooth surface. Then you could colourwash it in a soft Scandinavian shade or, if you are fairly artistic, you could paint it with a Scandinavian-influenced decoration.

Try not to hang coats on view in the hall – they almost always look untidy. It is much better to build a cupboard for coats and outerwear if you can; a cluttered look is not typically Scandinavian! It is also so much more welcoming for guests if there is somewhere to hang their coats that is not conspicuously temporary, such as being hung on the end of the bannisters.

Don't waste any space in your hall; the blind ends of corridors and nooks and crannies on landings can provide space for all kinds

By replacing the upper panels of an interior door with glass, you will let more daylight into the hall, thus maximizing natural light.

of purposes. Perhaps you can make a tiny reading area beside a bookshelf by adding a chair and lamp. If there is a bit more room, add a desk, and you have a study or home office. If you have a particularly large landing, perhaps you could put your dining table here, thus freeing up another room for a different use. Or, what about installing a tiny bathroom, or a least a shower. And you can never have enough storage; you could build a large cupboard in any odd corner of a landing.

ACCESSORIES

The hall is a good place to hang pictures; corridors and stairwells, particularly, are perfect for showing off sets or series of pictures. Do make sure, though, that they cannot be knocked off by people coming up or down the stairs; hanging them on just one wall will avoid a sense of overcrowding.

Flowers or plants make good accessories for the hall. Apart from looking lovely and welcoming, they will also perfume the hall. If your hall is too dark to support a real plant, try a dried flower arrangement or something artificial, and put bowls of pot pourri next to it. Alternatively, you could hang up a wreath of dried herbs or flowers. All these extras add to the sense of welcome and homecoming that your hall imparts.

$\mathcal{P}$ROJECTS

SANDED FLOORBOARDS

The warm, living appearance of a polished wooden floor will impart a Scandinavian feel to any room. Make sure that the floorboards are in sufficiently good condition to make an attractive floor. It is not worth trying to strip a floor with badly stained boards, mismatched planks or large gaps.

You will need

- Screwdriver and screws
- Countersink
- Hammer
- Floor nails
- Nail punch
- Wood filler
- Wide masking tape
- Face mask or handkerchief
- Large floor sander
- Coarse-, medium-, and fine-grade sandpaper

- Edging sander or handscraper (for edges and corners)
- Dry cloth
- Lint-free cloth
- Sealant, varnish or wood stain
- Paint roller
- 75mm (3in) paintbrush

1 *Remove all furniture from the room, and vacuum the floor thoroughly. Secure all loose floorboards, being careful to follow the lines of the joists underneath. Screws will give a better grip than nails, especially on warped boards; countersink the heads beneath the surface. Hammer the nails in well with the nail punch.*

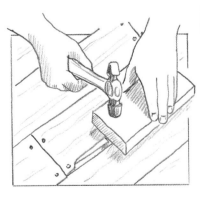

2 *Fill screwholes, small holes and fine cracks with wood filler; larger gaps can be filled with slivers of wood. Hammer these into position, using an offcut of wood to prevent the sliver from being damaged when you are hammering it.*

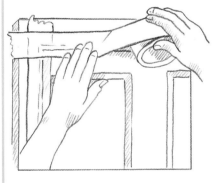

3 *Seal all the doors of the room with masking tape to prevent the dust permeating the entire house. Wear a face mask or tie a damp handkerchief around your nose and mouth. It is also a good idea to wear protective overalls and a close-fitting hat – a showercap is ideal.*

continued over ➤

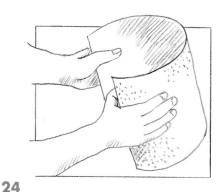

4 Fit the sander with coarse-grade sandpaper; rolling the sandpaper between your hands will make it easier to fit into the machine. Before switching the sander on, tilt it back on its wheels to lift the drum off the floor; switch it on and gently lower it onto the floor. Allow the sander to move forwards slowly, controlling its progress carefully. Do not try to hold it still or it will dig into the floor and create grooves.

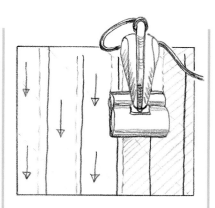

6 Fit medium-grade sandpaper in the machine and work up and down the room along the grain of the floorboards. Repeat with fine-grade sandpaper. Now, using the edging sander or handscraper, work on the corners and edges, starting with medium-, then finishing with fine-grade sandpaper.

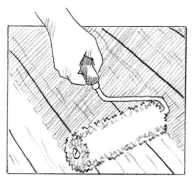

8 If you want to stencil the floor, this is the time to do it. If not, apply a coat of sealant with a paint roller, to make sure it sinks well into the boards. Leave to dry completely. Subsequent coats can be applied with a paintbrush, leaving each one to dry thoroughly. You will need two coats in rooms with rugs, three in a heavy traffic area such as a hall. Then replace the furniture and enjoy your new room!

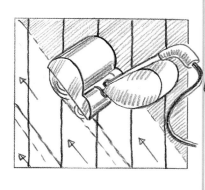

5 Work diagonally across the floor, raising the sander about 5cm (2in) before you reach the skirting board. Draw the sander slowly backwards to the starting point and repeat, overlapping sanded strips by about 7.5cm (3in). Then sand diagonally across the floor again in the opposite direction. Vacuum the floor.

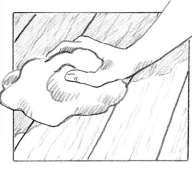

7 Vacuum thoroughly, then remove all traces of dust by wiping the floor with a dry cloth, shaking the cloth outside frequently. Then go over the floor again with a damp lint-free cloth. Leave overnight, then, if more dust has settled, wipe over it again with the dry cloth.

COLOURWASHED WOOD

This effect is subtle, smart and very Scandinavian-looking. It can be carried out on new and bare wood to impart, as the name implies, a gentle wash of colour, while the grain is still visible. It is equally effective over a solid pale colour; the delicate hint of translucent colour is very attractive. For woodwork, it is a good idea to protect the finish with two or three coats of matt polyurethane varnish.

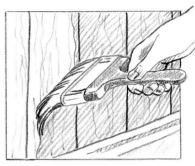

You will need

- Emulsion paint
- Clean empty yogurt pot
- Teaspoon
- Water
- 2.5cm (1in) paintbrush
- Paper or wood offcut for testing colours
- Paint kettle
- 10cm (4in) paintbrush
- Matt polyurethane varnish (optional)

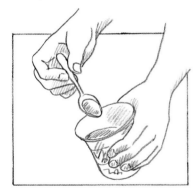

1 Put four teaspoonfuls of emulsion paint in the yogurt pot. Add two teaspoons of water and mix it well. Using the smaller paintbrush, test the colour on a piece of paper as close in tone to your background colour as possible. Alternatively, if your project is on new wood, test the colour on an offcut of wood.

2 Add two more teaspoons of water, stir and test again, then add two more, mix and test again. The more the paint is diluted, the fainter and more subtle the colour is going to be. Decide which tone you prefer; if in doubt, it is better to choose a paler one as you can always paint over it!

3 Having made your choice, tip the emulsion into the paint kettle and add the relevant proportion of water to dilute it. Stir the resulting mixture thoroughly.

4 Apply the paint over the wood, using the wide brush in large up-and-down strokes, finishing each time with a single sweep upwards to avoid any runs or drips. When dry, apply one or two coats of varnish, if appropriate; follow the manufacturer's instructions.

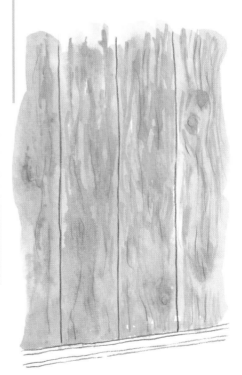

CHAPTER THREE

DINING ROOMS

EATING IS A PLEASURABLE OCCUPATION. It is not just the actual consumption of food that is, of course, pleasant; it is the sociable aspect of eating which is so enjoyable. There's no better place to enjoy the company of family and friends than over a relaxed, unhurried meal. So, if you are lucky enough to have a separate dining room in your house, you can really have fun making it the ideal Scandinavian-style room to eat in.

One of the most elegant of Swedish styles is that inspired by the Gustavian period. It seems to be particularly relevant to dining rooms, as many of today's furniture manufacturers are basing their newest designs on influences from that period. Or, if you prefer, you can create the more rustic look of old-fashioned Scandinavian farmhouses, with chunky furniture, and a more homespun, cosy feel.

1 *Soft yellow walls with a simple, understated pattern*
2 *Quarry tiles – another natural material – make a good choice for flooring*
3 *Simple cotton tie blinds blend with the wallpaper*
4 *Gustavian-style daybed and* straight-backed dining chairs, all painted in Scandinavian blue
5 *Three tablecloth fabrics give a farmhouse touch*
6 *Dried herb wreath and the open shelves with edging add to the rustic feel*

Or you can use the sleek lines of contemporary modern furniture, perhaps in beautiful pale wood or gleaming white, coupled with chairs of an almost architectural starkness.

WALLS AND CEILINGS

For a Gustavian feel, choose pale walls with a colourwashed effect and/or panels, either real or false. You could add texture to the walls by attaching narrow planks or wooden beading to them, to create a panelled effect, then paint the whole wall in the same colour. Cream is warm, but pale blue or grey is very Scandinavian, and creates a calm atmosphere in which to enjoy your food and company. Or, if you are artistic, you could paint *trompe l'oeil* panels.

For a less formal look, you could decorate your walls with an understated stencil pattern, either applied randomly or, to break up a large expanse of wall, arranged to form a border or dado rail, or even panels on the walls. Stencils could also form smart frames to surround your pictures. However, you may still prefer the simple, uncomplicated look of plain white walls. Choose the elements of Scandinavian design which suit you.

FLOOR

Sanded polished floorboards are still one of the best looking of floor coverings, for whatever style of Scandinavian decoration you have chosen. It is also practical for a dining room, if you have sealed them properly as spills can be wiped up quite easily. If you prefer, however, you could use ceramic tiles and add a runner or a couple of rugs, which will help to absorb sound.

WINDOWS

If you enjoy having formal dinner parties, curtains (or some form of window covering, such as a blind) are important in a dining room. You will need to draw them against the darkness of night, to achieve a sense of intimacy and to absorb some of the sound and chatter. But, in a Scandinavian-style dining room, curtains do not need to be elaborate; plain, gathered headings, and straightforward curtains

will look right, in a natural fabric, either plain and unpatterned or with an uncomplicated design such as a check.

You could soften the top of the window with a simple drape of fabric, designed to complement your particular Scandinavian style. If you favour Gustavian decoration, you could have a fairly sophisticated swag using swathes of fabric arranged through special curtain hoops (see page 34). If you have chosen a more countrified farmhouse feel, a simple piece of fabric thrown over either end of a plain curtain pole would look good. A cotton fabric with a strong, bold design would make lovely curtains for a modernist dining area.

A supremely elegant dining room in the Gustavian manner, complete with chandelier. The restrained colour scheme is warmed by the pink curtains.

LIGHTING

Artificial lighting is very important in a dining room because, as in the living room, the successful manipulation of light and shade is how you create atmosphere. In a dining room, you need all kinds of moods. You will need one ambience for a family high tea and another for a casual supper for lots of friends, or for a small, sophisticated dinner party. Adequate background light is essential, so that you can see what you are doing, coupled with accent lighting, such as recessed spotlights. These can be directed to illuminate specific areas, such as the table or a special painting, so that people can see what they are eating without being bathed in a glare of over-bright light.

The mellow wood, chunky lines and gingham curtains are typical elements of Scandinavian rustic-style decoration, allowing one to dine in light and comfort.

Candles are superb here, as they throw such warm and flattering light; put several on the table, but make sure that they do not stand at eye height as it is so difficult talking to the other guests with candlelight in your eyes! Hanging one or more mirrors with integral candlesticks on the wall would be ideal, as would siting table lamps where you want a bit more glow.

FURNITURE

Since the furniture in a dining room is so dominant, your choice of furniture will dictate the style of the room as a whole. It would be uncomfortable to have sophisticated panelled walls along with rustic heavy wood furniture; make sure the whole room is coherent for the style you choose.

In a dining room you will need somewhere to store china, glassware, and so on. A sideboard unit provides a wonderful amount of storage space, and is useful when serving meals. Look out for something that is relevant for your chosen Scandinavian style. There are several versions of Gustavian-style furniture available that are ideal for dining rooms: sideboards, glass-fronted display cabinets, and so on, to match tables and chairs. If your dinner service is attractive, it would look elegant laid out on view in a cupboard with glass doors, along with your glassware.

Pine sideboards are easily available if you prefer a farmhouse look. The warm glow of natural wood looks lovely, but you could paint the furniture if you wished, in a Scandinavian colour such as grey, cream or blue. Glass-fronted cupboards might jar a bit, unless they are quite solid. Open shelves are an option too, but take care that the contents of the shelves are interesting and well-ordered and not untidily piled up.

The other kind of Scandinavian look – the sleek modernist, slightly austere look – is not difficult to achieve. Keep to clean and unfussy designs, with everything very simple. Choose white or blonde wood furniture with plain lines; there is a good selection available.

Wall-hung plate racks would be pertinent to a dining room, and there are options for either a specific rack or set of open shelves for whichever Scandinavian style of decoration you favour. Shelves with classic Gustavian lines and ornamentation, modern understated glass, or, for farmhouse style, old-style dressers, would all look attractive in the right settings.

ACCESSORIES

The dining room is a good place to hang pictures; put them at the right height for diners to be able to see them well. If you are choosing a new dinner service, your style of dining room is relevant to your choice. If you have a sleek modern room, opt for simple glassware and white china. If you go for Gustavian, choose traditional, elegant designs. Peasant style needs more earthy, chunky crockery.

Finally, fresh flowers are, of course, always lovely but avoid strongly perfumed ones in a dining room as the scent will interfere with the flavour of the food. Evergreen plants are probably best as they always add freshness.

This contemporary dining room with its array of different materials and textures makes a pleasing and coherent whole.

$\mathcal{P}$ROJECTS

PADDED SEAT WITH FRILL

Most of the hardbacked chairs in Swedish artist Carl Larsson's turn-of-the-century home had seat cushions tied on them. Those in his living room had attractively frilled versions, which add an air of comfort and relaxation. So follow his lead and make some for your own chairs. A padded cushion makes a dining chair so much more comfortable; it softens a chair in a bedroom too.

You will need

- For each seat, a flat squab cushion to fit
- Piece of paper slightly bigger than the squab
- Pencil
- Tape measure
- Scissors
- Fabric; see step 1 for how to measure
- Matching thread
- Sewing machine
- Pins

1 Put the squab cushion on the paper and draw around it, adding 2cm (¾in) turnings all around. You will need two pieces of fabric this size. Measure around the edge of the pattern; for the frill, you will need a strip of fabric one and a half times that measurement, with 15cm (6in) extra for turnings, 25cm (10in) wide. For the ties, you will need a piece of fabric measuring 51 x 40cm (20 x 14in).

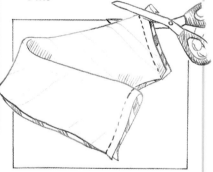

2 Cut out the fabric as listed in step 1. Measure the back edge of the squab, and cut off a section of the frill one and a half times that size. Fold it in half lengthways, with right sides together, and sew up the two sides with 12mm (½in) seams. Clip the seam corners, turn inside out and press. Repeat with the long frilled section of the frill.

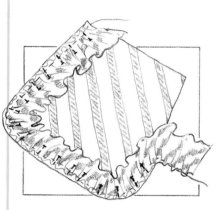

3 Run one loose gathering thread along both the raw edges of the long frill section; pull it up to fit around the front and sides of the squab. With right sides together, pin the frill to the sides and front edges of one of the seat pieces, leaving the back bare. Tack down.

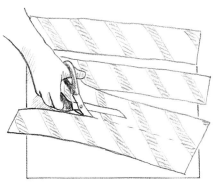

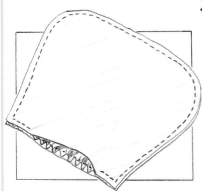

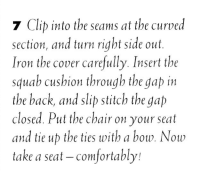

4 *Repeat with the back section; pin it in position on the back of the seat piece, leaving enough space to take the two supports of the chair-back and tack. Now make the ties. Cut four strips 9cm (3½in) wide from the piece measuring 51cm (20in) long. Fold one in half along the length, with right sides facing, and pin and sew along the long edge with a 12mm (½in) seam.*

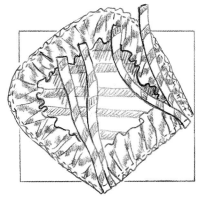

5 *Turn inside out and press, then turn in one end and slip stitch to close. Repeat with the other three ties. Take two of the ties and position them in the gap between the two frilled sections so that they can be tied around the chair-back easily. Pin the raw end of one tie to the edge of the seat piece, with the length of the tie inside.*

6 *Repeat with the other three and tack them in place. Lay the other seat piece on top, right-side down, sandwiching all the frills and ties. Pin everything together, and sew it with a 2cm (¾in) seam, taking care not to catch any frills or ties in the wrong place, and leaving a gap at the back.*

7 *Clip into the seams at the curved section, and turn right side out. Iron the cover carefully. Insert the squab cushion through the gap in the back, and slip stitch the gap closed. Put the chair on your seat and tie up the ties with a bow. Now take a seat – comfortably!*

SWAGGED CURTAIN HEADING

This window treatment adds elegance and sophistication to any Gustavian-style room. It is particularly good for dining rooms, as it softens the edge of the window while improving the acoustics of the room, helping to absorb excess noise in the room due to the resonant nature of the bare floorboards.

You will need

- Newspaper (joined together to make a large sheet)
- Tape measure
- Pencil
- Scissors
- Fabric
- Pins
- Matching thread
- Sewing machine
- Touch-and-close tape, the

width of the window
- Timber batten, the width of the window
- 2 or 3 x 4cm (1½in) wood screws
- PVA glue
- Screwdriver
- Pair of curtain valance loops, plus fitments

2 *Fold the pattern in half along line C–D and cut out both sides together to ensure they are identical. For the side pieces, you will need a rectangle of fabric about half the width of the window, and approximately two-thirds its length. You will need four pieces this size (two for each side), and two of the swag patterns; cut them out.*

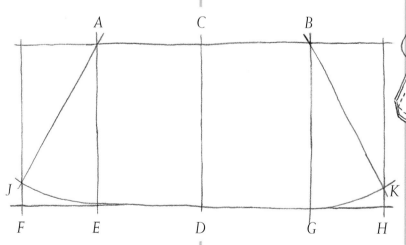

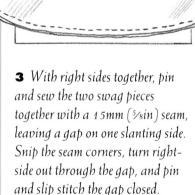

1 *Using the newspaper, make a pattern for the swag section. Measure the width of the window; this is line A–B. Line C–D measures approximately one-third of the depth of the window; lines E–F and G–H are about one-third*

the window's width. The lines A–J and B–K and lines A–E and B–G are the same length as line C–D, with a curve joining points E–J and K–G.

3 *With right sides together, pin and sew the two swag pieces together with a 15mm (⅝in) seam, leaving a gap on one slanting side. Snip the seam corners, turn right-side out through the gap, and pin and slip stitch the gap closed. Press, then pin the soft side of the touch-and-close tape along the back of the top edge of the swag; machine stitch into place.*

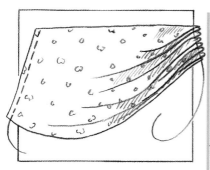

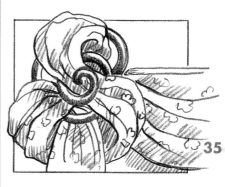

4 Run a line of gathering thread along the slanting sides of the swag; pull them up so that the swag measures about one-third of its original length. Instead of gathering, you may prefer to fold this up in small pleats which you pin in position as you go; then run a line of stitching across the whole thing.

6 Pin two pieces of the side section together, right sides facing. Sew them together with a 15mm (⅝in) seam, leaving a gap on one short side. Turn right side out through the gap, and press. Pin the gap closed, then slip stitch it and press. Repeat with the other side.

7 Hang the side pieces by feeding them through the hoops from the back; pull them through until you are left with a section about one-third of the depth of the window. Form knots or rosettes of fabric by coiling the fabric through the hoops around itself and pushing the end back through the hoops. Experiment until you like the look; if necessary, add some unseen stitches to hold the effect in place.

5 Attach the batten to the top of the window frame with the screws and glue the rough touch-and-close tape along it. Hang the swag in place by pressing both parts of the touch-and-close together; drape it to your satisfaction. Screw the curtain hoops on either side of the batten, following the manufacturer's directions.

CHAPTER FOUR

*L*IVING ROOMS

AS ITS NAME SUGGESTS, 'LIVING' IS WHAT GOES ON IN LIVING ROOMS. So to create a successful and stress-free living room for all the family, a lot of different activities need to be considered and planned for. How you choose to decorate it comes later.

First, you will want to sit and relax in your living room; comfortable chairs are therefore important. If your television is in the living room, you will need to be able to see that comfortably, with sufficient room for the whole family to watch it together. If a member of the family pursues a hobby in this room – knitting, model-making, embroidery, stamp-collecting, or whatever – the furniture arrangement needs to accommodate that, with adequate lighting and storage. The living room might be where you and friends and family play board games or cards. And, if you are

1 *Cool blue walls with white ceiling*
2 *Blonde wood parquet, relieved by geometric rug*
3 *Sheer fabric, strung on wire*
4 *Stylish table lamps and standard lamps*

5 *Comfortably squashy sofas and practical colour-matched shelving*
6 *Monchromatic, understated contents of shelves*

musical, does a large instrument such as a piano or double bass need space in the living room?

Your living room might also double up as your dining room; in that case, you will need dining furniture and space to store all the crockery, glassware, and so on. Perhaps the children do their homework here, or play with their toys or the computer under your watchful eye; if so, a suitable table and chairs are necessary, if your dining table is elsewhere.

Having taken into account all this flexibility of purpose for your living room, now you can plan its Scandinavian design. And, in fact, this style of decoration lends itself beautifully to living rooms; the restrained colours and elegant simplicity are ideal for creating a restful and relaxed atmosphere.

WALLS AND CEILING

A pale colour for walls, or perhaps a small all-over pattern, again in subtle shades, are best for a Scandinavian feel. In a living room, you can afford to make a bit more of the texture of your walls by creating a panelled effect, with either real or fake panelling. Old panelling is sometimes available from salvage yards, or you could attach shallow planks or beading to the wall in a uniform pattern to look like panels – either floor to ceiling size, or higher on the walls like large picture frames. Painting the complete result in the same light tone – a warm creamy white, for example – will look very Nordic. If you like, you could colourwash over that with a soft shade.

If you are fairly artistic you could create *trompe l'oeil* panels with paint, or prepare wonderful painted panels in the Gustavian manner. Such panels could be edged in painted mouldings with a pretty interior border of foliage or flowers, and interwoven with ribbon. It would offset Gustavian-style furniture to perfection. You could also fake these panels by choosing a wallpaper border with a similar pattern and putting panels on the walls, mitring the corners.

If you wanted to create a more casual, Nordic farmhouse style, you could line the walls with tongue-and-groove boards and paint these in a plain, pastel colour. You could even stencil or paint them

all over with folk-type designs for a very individual Scandinavian look. For a modernist look, simple smooth white walls are all that are needed.

FLOOR

Stripped wooden floorboards are the most authentic Scandinavian floorcovering, perhaps with a colourwashed or limed finish. You can then add some colour and pattern with rugs. The most valid kind of rugs would be long narrow runners, usually made of woven cotton, but occasionally wool. However, wooden floorboards might be a little noisy with all the comings and goings in a living room, even with the addition of rugs. So, for your Scandinavian look, you could cheat just a tiny bit and put down a natural covering such as sisal or coir, or even neutral-coloured carpet, which would impart a similar natural feel. You could then add rugs on top!

This exuberant peasant-style decoration features stencils and hand-painted patterns on the tongue-and-groove boarding. The comfortable wooden furniture blends into the style beautifully.

Blonde wood and a rosy red carpet, coupled with wonderful windows, create a bright modernist living room. The tidy and orderly contents of the shelves add to the cool, uncluttered feel.

WINDOWS

As much daylight as possible was required in traditional Scandinavian interiors, so curtains tended not to be elaborate, if indeed they were there at all. Exterior wooden shutters and, occasionally, interior ones, kept warmth in during winter; they still look very good today. Nowadays, with electric illumination, it is unnecessary to live by the pattern of the sun; and in our overcrowded towns we often need curtains, or at least blinds, to hide an ugly view or give privacy if the room is overlooked. But, to achieve a fairly accurate Scandinavian look, your living room curtain treatment should be as simple and unfussy as possible.

Curtains should be unlined cotton, with a softly coloured,

small pattern, perhaps checked or with narrow stripes, or an unelaborate all-over design. Alternatively, use a sheer fabric which lets light through. The heading could be an unfussy pencil pleat, simple grip-hooks, or matching fabric tabs over an iron curtain pole.

For a more rustic look, you could have café curtain scallops hung from a wooden pole, or simply a sheer or plain, fine cotton curtain stretched on expandable curtain wire. To soften the angles of a window, you could hang a pleated frill as a pelmet just over the top edge. Draping some fabric loosely over a pole, or through special curtain hooks, would have the same effect.

LIGHTING

The manipulation of artificial lighting is important in helping to exploit the living room and use it to the full. It is usually in the evening that all the family are gathered to pursue their own interests, so the lighting system in the living room must enable them to do that. It is possible – indeed, it is fairly easy – to choose flexible lighting options that still reflect Scandinavian influences.

With the long Scandinavian winter, artificial light was and is of great significance. In the days before electric light, candles and tapers were vital and, to increase the effect, mirrors were sometimes made with a candlestick in front, to reflect as much light from the flame as possible. In the late 18th century, mirror-maker Nicolas

An elegant living room, complete with firelight and candlelight (note the mirror with its integral candlesticks) to bring it to life. The furniture is a mix of Gustavian influence and modern comfort.

Meunier, working in Stockholm, made many such decorative mirrors with integral single or double candle-holders. These are now being reproduced for today's market, and are just the thing for background and mood light in your Scandinavian living room – whether or not you have chosen Gustavian or peasant style. Do keep an eye on the candles, though. You could also use intricately moulded glass chandeliers for a Gustavian feel. Of course, unobtrusive light fittings will also work perfectly well in your Nordic-style room – wall-hung uplighters are best, as they throw gentle and flattering light.

For more concentrated illuminations for reading or sewing, lamps are very useful. Choose tall candlestick-style bases in pale colours; the shade can then be either a small pleated version in gingham or similar checked fabric, or you can easily make a very Scandinavian pierced shade which lets a delicate pattern of light through. White is best, although off-white or cream are good too (see page 45).

FIREPLACE

Modern Scandinavian homes are built with superb insulation so, in spite of the cold winters, the houses are very warm. But a major decorative item in Scandinavian living rooms, particularly Swedish ones, is the fire or stove, which dates from the turn of the 18th century. If you can have an open fireplace, it will go a long way to adding Scandinavian style to your room, especially if it is architecturally interesting in its own right, with no focus on the mantelpiece or fire surround. Alternatively, a decorative, free-standing cast-iron stove will add Scandinavian character, particularly to a more rustic, peasant-style interior.

FURNITURE

It depends on how much space you have as to how much furniture you can fit in your living room. Obviously you want to have enough chairs for all the family so that you can all sit down together. For a Scandinavian feel, choose unfussy lines and pale fabrics for the upholstery. A cot-style sofa is ideal, and it can even double up as a bed for overnight guests. Washable loose covers, or at least some kind of stain-resistant treatment for the fabric, would be very practical.

Storage is important in a living room; providing sufficient cupboard space cuts down on visible clutter and gives the room a cleaner, restrained look, important for Scandinavian style. There are several versions of Gustavian-style glass-fronted cupboards on the market. If you have pretty things and can arrange them well, this is an excellent option; if you are inclined to be untidy, go for cupboard doors that are solid, or line the glass doors with fabric.

Built-in units can often make the best use of space, and you can tailor-make them for what you have to store. Choose pale wood for your units, or paint them all off-white. Bookshelves, as long as the books are arranged neatly, look great and indeed help to give a comfortable lived-in look to the room.

Tables – coffee tables, side tables and even dining tables – need to be kept tidy too, unless, of course, they are actually in use. To

This simple pierced paper lampshade looks very cool and stylish, yet is easy to make at home using cardboard and needles.

have a coherent interior, it helps if they and other occasional furniture are all made from the same material and/or colour.

ACCESSORIES

As for any room, the accessories you choose for your living room add your own individual character and comfort. But take care with a Scandinavian-influenced decor that your accessories are not over-done and higgledy-piggledy, but tone with the understated colour schemes and have a sense of being an integral part of the whole room.

Cushions are useful for adding comfort to any room; a pile on a sofa, for example, provides a satisfying sense of luxury. They don't have to look fussy, though; choose plain and unfrilled ones for a Scandinavian feel.

Pictures must be chosen and framed carefully to enhance the soft tones and restful feel of the room. The same goes for a collection of family photos. Whether hung on the wall or arranged on a surface, these would be fine as long as the frames all match, and those frames are of a pastel colour or blonde wood to blend with the room as a whole. A mishmash of frames of different colours and materials would jar uncomfortably with the rest of your Scandinavian interior. Plaster wall plaques or busts in the classical manner will underline a Gustavian character, as would delicate plate racks displaying dishes with 18th-century patterns.

Plants and flowers always add life and freshness to a living room, or indeed any room. While they cannot really jar as such, it is still best to choose colours and shapes carefully. Elaborate floral arrangements with lots of different colours and flowers will not look as good as a bunch of one type of blooms, preferably pastel-coloured or, even better, white. Evergreen trailing plants such as ivy or jasmine are excellent; training them around a wire ball gives a very Swedish touch.

$\mathcal{P}$ROJECTS

PIERCED LAMPSHADE

A white table lampshade, pierced with a design of tiny holes to let a twinkling pattern of light shine through, makes a lovely cool statement like the star-filled Nordic sky. Making your own is very easy – why not have a go. This is a coolie-style lampshade, with a 10cm (4in) top diameter, a 25cm (10in) bottom diameter, and 15cm (6in) high. Do not use a light bulb more powerful than 40 watts.

You will need

❋

- 2 sheets of thin white card, 30 x 50cm (12 x 20in)
- Pencil
- Ruler
- String, 50cm (20in) long
- Drawing pin
- Craft knife
- Cork board, for pressing on
- Thimble
- Sharp needles of various sizes

- Tracing paper
- Fine-grade sandpaper
- Pegs
- Top lampshade ring, 10cm (4in) in diameter, with an attached gimbal ring (an inner ring on two arms), 25cm (10in) in diameter
- Glue
- White bias binding
- Lampbase

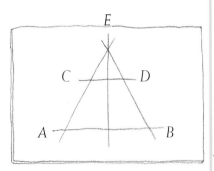

1 *Take one sheet of card for the pattern. Draw a line down the centre of the card, then draw a perpendicular line 25cm (10in) long (which is the bottom diameter of the shade). Label the line A–B. Draw another line 10cm (4in) long (the top diameter), positioned 15cm (6in) above A–B; label this line C–D. Now draw line A–E, through point C, and line B–E, through point D.*

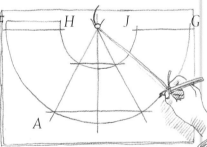

2 *Attach one end of the string to the drawing pin, and insert its point at E. Stretch the string to point A and tie the pencil there. Use it to draw arc F–G, and then draw arc H–J. Join the arcs with lines F–H and J–G, adding 2cm (¾in) for a seam overlap along one edge. Cut out the pattern and lay the cut-out pattern on the board.*

3 *Now put on the thimble and experiment with piercing a design through the card using the drawing pin and needles. Try using needles with different-sized points, holding the pattern up to a naked light bulb to see the effect*

continued over ➤

until you create a motif you like; a fairly small pattern is probably best. Repeat it around the bottom edge of the shade, and around the top as well, if you like. An all-over pattern might be a bit much!

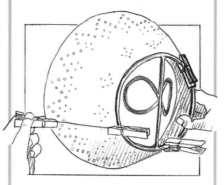

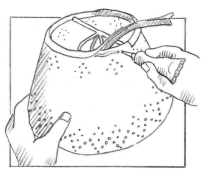

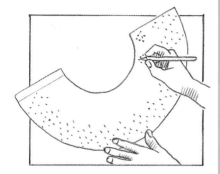

4 Having decided on your final design, place the pattern on top of the other sheet of card, and trace around it carefully. Cut out the shade and place it right-side up on the cork. Lightly draw out your design for piercing in pencil, and execute it with care. When complete, turn the shade over to the wrong side, and gently rub it with the fine-grade sandpaper to smooth out the projections left from piercing.

5 Make up the shade by rolling the card into a shade shape, carefully easing it slowly into a roll shape to prevent creasing. Peg the top ring into position and ease the bottom until the diameter is 25cm (10in) across. Mark the seam overlap line with pencil, then take off the pegs and glue the seam in place, holding with pegs.

6 When dry, put a line of glue round the top fitting and stick the shade in position, holding it with pegs until dry. Trim the top edge of your lamp with bias binding, sticking it neatly in place over the raw edge of the card and the top ring. When dry, fix your new shade on a suitable lampbase — for a Scandinavian look, a tall white candlestick-type base is best.

CUSHION WITH TAILORED TRIM

Cushions are useful for adding comfort and a touch of colour to any room. They do not have to look fussy, though. For your Scandinavian interior, opt for plain ones, or ones like this box-edged version for a smart tailored look.

You will need

- Scissors
- 1m (40in) fabric, 90cm (36in) wide, or 0.5m (20in) fabric, 122cm (48in) wide
- Tape measure
- Pins
- Zip, 30cm (12in) long
- Thread
- Ruler
- Tailor's chalk
- 150cm (5ft) cord trim (optional)
- Cushion pad, 35cm (13¾in) square

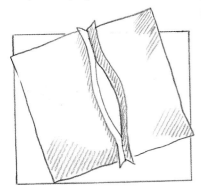

1 *Cut one piece of fabric 50cm (19½in) square, and another 50 x 53cm (19½ x 21in). Cut the longer piece in half along its shorter side, then pin these two pieces together with right sides facing. Leaving a 30cm (12in) gap in the centre for the zip, sew the two pieces together with a 2cm (¾in) seam at each end.*

2 *To insert the zip, lay the joined pieces of fabric flat, wrong side up, and press open the seam allowance. Pin and tack the zip centrally over the seam allowance and between the machine stitching; sew in place. Press again, then with right sides facing, pin the cushion pieces together. Sew them with a 2cm (¾ in) seam, taking care to make the corners as near to right angles as possible.*

3 *Clip the corners of the seam allowance and press the seams as flat as possible. Turn the cushion right side out and press again.*

Next, using tailor's chalk and a ruler, mark a border 5cm (2in) towards the centre, making it as precise as you can; it is better that the internal cushion should be a little misshapen than to have a crooked border.

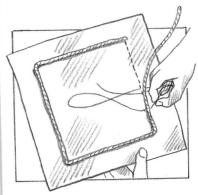

4 *Tack along the marked border, then run a line of machine stitching along the tacking. If you like, you can then emphasize the stitching by machine sewing with thicker contrasting thread, or by sewing decorative cord along the row of stitching. Finally insert the cushion pad.*

CHAPTER FIVE

Kitchens

49

THERE IS A GREAT SENSE OF PURPOSE IN A KITCHEN. It is the factory of the house: basic materials (foodstuffs) are turned into a different end product (meals), with all the side effects that such a manufacturing process entails, such as preparation areas, washing up, and so on. In addition, the kitchen is the real heart of the house and everything else goes on in there.

It is difficult to make a kitchen work well if it is badly arranged. Scandinavian principles of design mean that efficient planning is of outstanding importance, particularly in a functional room such as a kitchen. But before you dash off to plan an expensive new kitchen from scratch, have a look at your existing one to see whether you can reorganize it to alleviate the problems.

Perhaps it is too small. Could you resite something like the

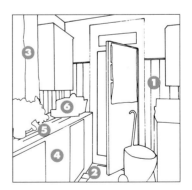

1 *Tongue-and-groove panelling on the walls, painted off-white*
2 *Stripped floorboards in limed wood, softened with a woven rag runner*
3 *Simple, unlined checked curtains strung on wire*
4 *Kitchen units colourwashed with a translucent beige film*
5 *Scrubbed wooden draining board and work surface*
6 *Accessories in different natural materials*

freezer, (perhaps it could go into a cupboard in the hall or even the spare room), or the washing machine (perhaps this could be replumbed in a bathroom). That should reduce the pressure on the kitchen, allowing you to spread out a bit more. If your work surfaces are bitty and stained, and don't utilize the space well, replanning them will help. Building a new worktop which runs along the whole length of your units will create a much more businesslike appearance in the kitchen; install shelves or put wheeled vegetable racks in any gaps underneath. If the units are in good condition but the colour is very dated, you could renew the appearance of the kitchen by painting the doors. Or if the design is adequate, but the doors are chipped and broken, you could hang new doors.

However, if the kitchen is beyond redemption, installing a brand new one, tailor-made for your needs, will probably increase the value of your house – and will certainly increase the quality of your life. But plan it carefully to accommodate everything you want from it; use Scandinavian principles of design, and think about form and function.

With a little more thought, it is quite easy to have a Scandinavian kitchen as well.

WALLS AND CEILING

As usual with Scandinavian styles, pale, restrained colours will help to achieve the look. Paint is a practical wallcovering, or you could choose a washable wallpaper with an understated pattern. For a rustic farmhouse feel, line the walls with tongue-and-groove weatherboarding, which you could stencil with pastel designs if you like. If you painted the tongue-and-groove glossy white, though, it would impart a modern sleekness, as would plain walls in matt white. Pale colourwashed walls would look faintly Gustavian; perhaps you could add *faux* panels.

FLOOR

The omnipresent stripped floorboards are particularly good for kitchens, as they are practical for keeping clean as long as they are

varnished properly. They are also resilient and warm underfoot, which makes it less tiring for the miles you tend to walk while preparing three meals a day!

You could add rugs for cosiness, but ensure that they are anchored with a material which will grip to the planks as well as possible, to avoid tripping over. As they tend to slide, it is not advisable to have rugs in the kitchen if you have young children or are elderly. Alternatively, a plain sheet vinyl or linoleum flooring in a neutral colour might be a more suitable solution for a very busy kitchen – floorboards could be rather noisy.

The glow of polished wood and the warmth of natural textures, together with details like the shelf edgings, combine to make this large and friendly kitchen the heart of the home.

The sludgy green shade of the varnish, a typically Scandinavian colour, sets off the beautifully-turned supports of this kitchen unit.

WINDOWS

Unembellished window treatments are appropriate for a kitchen with a Nordic feel. A blind is probably best; because it hangs at the top of the window, it adds interest to the window without cluttering up the work surface, and it does not get as dirty as a curtain. There are plenty of different kinds of blinds, from roller to Venetian; a variation on an Austrian blind would look good, and is easy to make (see page 74). For your Scandinavian-style kitchen, opt for a simple frilled curtain valance for a rustic feel, stark Venetian blinds for a contemporary look and a casual swag for Gustavian character.

LIGHTING

You need efficient lighting in a kitchen, whatever the style of its decorations; it is vital to see properly when you are slicing and chopping meat or vegetables. The best solution for lighting the work surfaces clearly is to have under-unit lighting which floods the worktop with light, but from which glare at eye level is prevented by a baffle in front of the light itself. For less specific illumination, for example during meal times, you could have a rise-and-fall pendant fitting or a table lamp in keeping in design with your chosen Scandinavian feel.

FURNITURE

The units are what makes a kitchen what it is, so, if you want a Nordic flavour in your new kitchen, choose your units with care. Plain and uncluttered doors with simple handles will work for whichever Scandinavian style you follow.

If your units are sound but outdated, you could paint the doors to give them a new Scandinavian lease of life; applying a soft pale colour, such as blue or cream, will immediately give the kitchen a more Nordic look. Colourwashing over white would look even better.

You could give units a Gustavian feel by gluing classical embellishments to plain doors, and painting the result in grey or faded blue. Or for an exuberant and unique peasant-style kitchen, you could stencil or even paint pictures or patterns on the units themselves.

If the frameworks of your kitchen units are sturdy enough, but the doors are chipped and broken, you could buy new doors. Clean-lined doors in blonde wood would look very modern, as would white ones, perhaps with a textured finish.

It is easy to make the other furniture in the kitchen fit in well with your interpretation of Scandinavian style. Sturdy pine tables with turned legs look best with a rustic style; classical-style tables with carved ornamentation on the legs and perhaps a beaded edging, with chairs to match, are just right for a Gustavian feel; while the clean-cut, smooth lines of modern design add to a contemporary kitchen. Dressers and open shelving can be fitted out in keeping with displays to match.

Blonde wood, blue walls and a well-planned arrangement of furniture, with everything to hand, are the perfect ingredients for a contemporary Nordic kitchen.

ACCESSORIES

The details in a kitchen accentuate its character, enhancing its individuality. If it is peasant style you favour, make accessories such as handcut paper lace edging on the open shelves, to heighten the rusticity (see page 54). Plaster wall plaques or busts in the classical manner will underline a Gustavian character, as would delicate plate racks displaying dishes with 18th-century patterns. For a more modern feel, place a single bowl or vase with a beautiful contemporary shape and design on an entire shelf.

If you find yourself inspired by the simplicity of any Scandinavian design – for crockery or otherwise – you could try recreating it loosely on a bowl or plate, and displaying it in your kitchen. It does not matter if it is not a particularly good replica; it will bring you pleasure, and it is not difficult to do (see page 56).

$\mathcal{P}$ROJECTS

DECORATIVE SHELF EDGE

This decorative lacy edging for shelves is inspired by the Scandinavian display cupboard (*fatehbur* in Norwegian), a common item in Nordic rustic homes. It was designed to be left open with the contents on view; the interior was often beautifully painted, and the shelves were decorated with tatted lace trim. You could brighten your rustic-style kitchen of today with handmade edgings of lacy paper; it would certainly help to enliven stark open shelves.

You will need

- Ruler
- Roll of baking parchment
- Pencil
- Sharp scissors
- Tea towel
- Iron
- Brass drawing pins

1 *Measure the width of the shelf (or shelves) you want to decorate. Cut a piece of baking parchment that width and about 15cm (6in) deep. Using the pencil and the ruler, divide the paper up into an even number of sections about 2.5cm (1in) wide. Fold it up precisely, concertina-style; but do not crease the folds too firmly.*

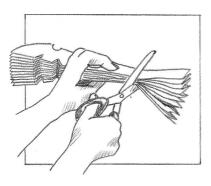

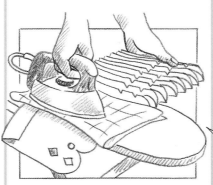

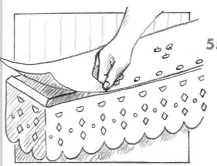

2 *Leave the top 5cm (2in) blank. Draw a curve along the lower edge and small geometric patterns along the folds of the parchment. Cut them out carefully with the scissors. Unfold the parchment and see the scalloped edge and lacy effect. You will probably want to try several times with new lengths of parchment, perfecting the motifs you like, until you are satisfied with your handiwork.*

3 *When you are happy with your paper lace, place it on the ironing board, cover it with a dry tea towel and press it with a warm iron, to diminish the effect of the folds. Now fold over the blank 5cm (2in) at the top along the complete length of the strip, creasing the fold precisely and carefully.*

4 *Hang that fold over the shelf, with the lacy section hanging over the edge. Cut another piece of baking parchment the size of the shelf itself, and lay the front edge over the edge of the lace. Anchor it down all around with evenly spaced drawing pins.*

KARELIAN BOWL

The decoration on this bowl is inspired by antique ceramic dishes from the province of Karelia, in eastern Finland. The very simplicity of the pattern is beautiful, and makes it easy to imitate. A series of painted bowls would look lovely displayed on a kitchen shelf or plate rack, giving a very Nordic air. You may find other Scandinavian designs you would like to recreate on crockery – enjoy experimenting!

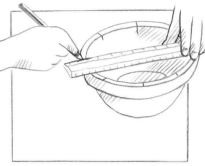

You will need

- Cake-icing carousel (optional)
- Old saucer
- Artist's fine brush
- Cream ceramic paint
- Glazed terracotta bowl
- Chinagraph pencil, or pen which will write on ceramic
- Ruler

1 *It is worth obtaining a carousel; it makes painting lines around the bowl so much easier as your hand stays still while the bowl moves, instead of vice versa. Borrow or hire one, if you can. Use the old saucer to try out the paint and practise different techniques; experiment with painting concentric circles while the saucer is turning on the carousel.*

2 *Take the terracotta bowl. With the chinagraph pencil, put a mark on the rim; use the ruler to put another mark directly opposite it, bisecting the bowl equally. Then divide those halves in half, with their opposites, continuing to divide the bowl into 16 sections. Extend these chinagraph marks 2.5cm (1in) inside the bowl. This will ensure the pattern is positioned reasonably straight and evenly.*

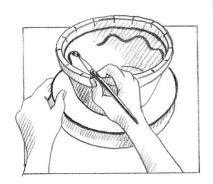

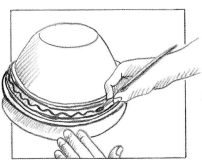

3 *Put the bowl on the carousel. Spin it slowly and, with a fully loaded paintbrush, draw a circle 2.5cm (1in) inside the bowl. Now load the brush again and paint the* wavy line. Relax while you are painting. It should not be too precise; the effect should be of freehand painting. Your guiding marks will prevent the line from waving about too erratically and ensuring that it will meet at the starting point.

4 *Now add the dots on either side of the wavy line. Turn the bowl over and paint a border with two concentric rings on the outer side, and another wavy line if you like. When you are happy with the result, leave the bowl to dry completely, or follow the manufacturer's instructions, as some ceramic paints need to 'cure' in a hot oven.*

Then if you like, you can decorate other bowls, to add to your display.

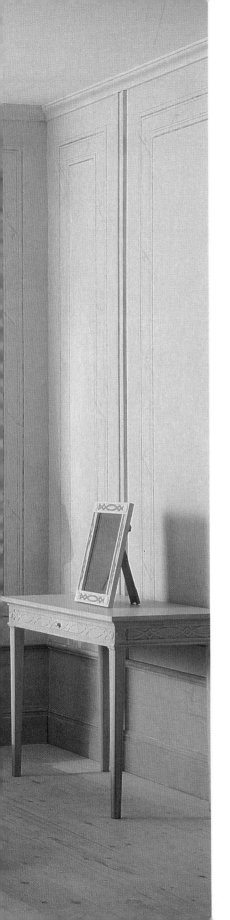

CHAPTER SIX

BEDROOMS

A BEDROOM IS MORE THAN JUST A PLACE TO SLEEP. It should represent a refuge, a place where you can escape from the pressures of everyday life, somewhere private and personal. Decorating a bedroom in a Scandinavian manner follows these criteria exactly. The calm and classic colour schemes, the plain, warm tones of flooring in natural materials, and the elegant and clean lines of furniture sound like a recipe for creating a tranquil haven. A bedroom with Scandinavian style has a serene atmosphere which is ideal for starting the day – and ending it – in a relaxed and positive state of mind.

WALLS AND CEILING

Soft subtle colours are best on bedroom walls. The dusky blues and greens so favoured by Scandinavians are particularly relaxing, but a

1 *Panelled walls with deep skirting boards in the 18th-century manner*
2 *Gustavian-style bed with elegant drapes*

3 *Colourwashed floorboards*
4 *Delicately painted bedside table, and classic carving on the footstool*

A canopied bed gives real privacy, accentuated by the warm but restrained colour scheme.

buttery-coloured cream would provide a cosy feel, especially if you painted the ceiling to match and reflect the light.

For a more interesting effect than flat-coloured walls, you could colourwash them, or apply an understated stencil to the walls, either randomly or so that the repeated stencilled motif forms a border at ceiling or waist height. Choose a tone just a little darker than that of the walls for your stencil so that it is not obtrusive.

If you prefer the peasant, cottage look, drawn from the traditions of the rural Scandinavian farming community, you could choose a wallpaper with an all-over 'hand-painted' design or perhaps paint your own freehand floral baskets, for example. If you are very creative, you could design your own *kurbitz* decoration.

FLOOR

As usual, stripped floorboards would look right in a room of the Scandinavian genre. But since bedrooms should be as insulated from noise and cold as possible, these are perhaps not the best idea for the realities of life. A more practical, and certainly more comfortable, solution, while still looking authentic, would be plain pale toffee-coloured carpet in a berber weave or hard-wearing woven sisal, jute or seagrass flooring.

WINDOWS

The windows in a bedroom need some method of obscuring the glass for night-time privacy, unless you live in the country miles away from any neighbours. For this reason, thin or sheer fabrics are not really adequate or suitable. If you especially like the look of draped muslin, you could have a swathe of this fabric camouflaging a roman blind in thick cotton fabric; if that cotton is of a check pattern, so much the better for a Nordic feel. Shutters, or Venetian or vertical blinds can help; the daylight filters through very attractively but you can close the slats at night for complete privacy. Full-length curtains are practical for insulation, as well as imparting a sense of luxury; in a bedroom, you can have them lined and interlined for warmth, if you like. Use a natural cotton or linen weave for a contemporary look, either plain or maybe with a woven texture to prevent blandness. Alternatively, fabric with a one-colour checked or striped pattern, in subtle tones on an unbleached cotton background, is ideal for a Scandinavian feel. These curtains should have a simple gathered heading, as being the best solution for keeping out the light of the dawning day.

If you favour the rustic peasant look, patchwork curtains would look great – and be great fun to make, as well.

LIGHTING

The manipulation of light – both daylight and artificial – is particularly important in a bedroom to create a relaxing atmosphere. You need efficient lamps to throw specific pools of light for reading in bed, or applying make-up and brushing hair, yet you also need an overall background glow to see when you are moving about. Table lamps or wall-hung lights are probably the best option – ceiling pendants tend to cast rather an overbright glare and it is easy to stand in your own light. There are plenty of fittings available which will fit in elegantly with your scheme. Candlelight is wonderfully romantic, especially if it is reflected in a mirror – but keep an eye on the lighted flame and take care to extinguish it properly.

FURNITURE

The bed is obviously the single most important item of furniture in a bedroom. Its design will contribute most directly to dictating the style of the whole room. So, for a Scandinavian bedroom, a bed with Scandinavian roots is a must. There are several options available. The most elegant would be to choose a bedstead with Gustavian-influenced carvings, with furniture to match or blend with it. The simplicity of line, coupled with the carvings with their mixture of rococo exuberance and classical symmetry, make for a fairly formal, yet fresh bedroom. Any bedroom needs bedside tables, cupboards, dressing tables, chests-of-drawers and other storage, of course, but for your Scandinavian Gustavian-style bedroom it is best to choose furniture in a similar vernacular to create a coherent interior. This style is currently enjoying a revival in popularity and quite a few versions are available on the market today.

Alternatively, you could choose a cot bed or trundle bed, based on beds found in rural farmhouses. Due to the lack of space in these cottages, these daybeds acted as sofas by day and pulled out to reveal beds at night. In their simplest form they were very rustic, hand-carved and often hand-painted with exuberant local decoration. As time went on, and some farmers became more affluent, the cot beds could often be found carved with great sophistication, with classical Gustavian carvings. For today's lifestyle, with space still being at a premium in our crowded towns, a daybed with cushions forms a very practical solution for a guest room. The room could then function well as a study or playroom, or TV room, until you actually have guests.

Alternatively, if you prefer, there are plenty of examples of contemporary Scandinavian style, with beds, often made of blonde

An uncluttered, well-planned
bedroom with a contemporary feel.
The smart box-pleated bedspread
adds to the tailored appearance.

wood with clean, uncluttered lines, which will help to create a smart sleeping haven for you.

Another method of focusing on the bed is to hang a drape or curtain over it. There are various ways of doing this, but a canopy hung over the bed is fairly simple to make and looks very effective (see page 64).

ACCESSORIES

Since the bed is the most dominant item in a bedroom, the bed linen will have a strong influence on the look. Choose white or softly natural colours for your bedcovers. Again, patterns are best kept subtly coloured; woven (or appliquéd or embroidered) one-coloured textures look very good. Crisp cotton or linen is perfect – equally relevant for a Gustavian or a contemporary feel, though for the latter a fitted pleated bedspread would add a smartly tailored appearance.

In a peasant-style bedroom, quilts, perhaps in fairly understated patchwork, would be in keeping, but so would linen or cotton. Other accessories should be kept to a minimum. Pictures are fine; it is better, though, to have one or two lovely works hanging on the walls than lots of family photos crowded on a surface. Avoid untidy storage such as hanging jewellery, belts or whatever, over the dressing table mirror or on the backs of chairs – put things away out of sight. Attractive boxes on tops of the wardrobes will look nice while providing unobtrusive extra storage.

$\mathcal{P}$ROJECTS

You will need

- 2 decorative curtain pole brackets, with fixings
- Screwdriver
- Tape measure
- Fabric for drape and tie-backs
- Scissors
- Pins
- Thread to match
- Sewing machine
- Curtain pole, approximately 53cm (15in) long, 4cm (1½in) in diameter
- Wooden finial painted to match the colour scheme
- 4 small brass rings and 2 hooks for tie-backs

BED CANOPY

Hanging a fabric drape over the bed adds importance and elegance to the whole room. There are plenty of ways of doing this, but here is one of the simplest. The drapes are hung on a short curtain pole suspended above the bed, and then held back by tie-backs at either side of the bed. You can choose a sheer fabric for an ethereal feel, or a lined cotton one for a more substantial appearance.

1 *Following the manufacturer's instructions, attach the two curtain brackets to the ceiling; ensure they are securely fixed to a ceiling joist.*

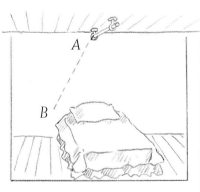

2 *Decide where you want to position the tiebacks – about 8cm (3in) from the edge of the mattress, and about 15cm (6in) above it is about right; allow clearance for a bedside table if desired. Measure from the top of the pole to the floor, passing through the tie-back position (line A–B).*

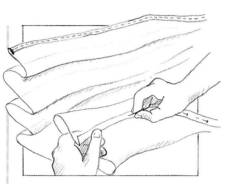

3 *Double this measurement if you are using an unlined sheer fabric, or quadruple it if the curtain needs to be lined to match. Add 24cm (9½in) to allow for draping and turnings, and add 7cm (3in) for tie-backs; also allow for any pattern repeat. This is the amount of fabric you need. If using a sheer fabric, turn in a 1cm (½in) hem along both selvedges and sew down.*

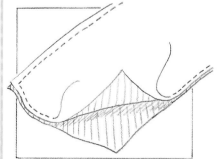

4 *To make the drape double-sided, so that no wrong side is visible, cut the fabric into two equal lengths,*

and lay them flat, right sides together. Pin both the long edges and one short edge, then sew them with a 1cm (½in) hem. If your fabric has a directional pattern, cut the long pieces again into two equal lengths, and join them together along three sides, making sure the pattern on all pieces runs the same way.

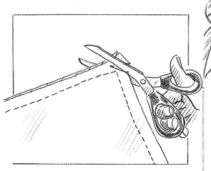

5 Turn the fabric right side out, snipping across seam corners to avoid bulk. Now fold the drape in half lengthways, and pin and sew a tube 6cm (2½in) from the fold, to form a casing for the pole. Turn in the raw short edge of the drape and slip stitch it.

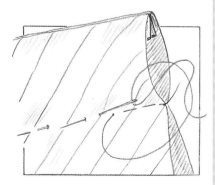

6 With a directional pattern, join both sections of the patterned pieces at raw edges with a 15mm (5/8in)

seam. Press the seam open, then fold the drape over the seam, with the seam allowance on the wrong side. Pin and sew a casing tube as described, with the seam inside.

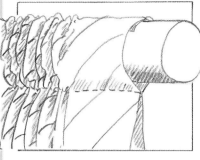

7 Feed the drape on to the pole, gathering it up as much as necessary. Put the pole into the first bracket, then put on the second bracket and attach it to its fixings. Add the finial.

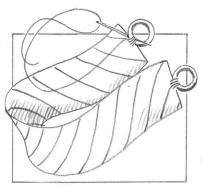

8 For the tie-backs, cut two strips of fabric 7cm (3in) wide and the desired length. Fold the fabric in half lengthways and join with a 15mm (5/8in) seam. Turn right side out and press. Turn in the raw edges on the short sides, incorporating a brass ring in the centre of each. Hang the hooks where you want to position the tie-backs, and drape your curtains to your satisfaction.

CHAPTER SEVEN

*B*ATHROOMS

BATHROOMS INFLUENCED BY THE PRINCIPLES of Scandinavian design are well organized and sleek. The colour scheme is cool and relaxed, featuring pastel tones and subtle, if any, pattern. The feeling is of a calm haven of privacy, vital for full enjoyment of a soothing bath, or an invigorating shower. There is nothing jarring or over-busy in here – even the accessories are simple, and the towels are unpatterned and pastel.

Creating a new-style bathroom, whether it is one with a Scandinavian feel or not, is difficult if your present bathroom is badly arranged. The very nature of a bathroom means that practical planning is paramount. If the lavatory in your existing bathroom is too close to the basin, or there is insufficient room to get in and out of the shower comfortably, you will never be able to turn this room

1 *Painted timber ceiling*
2 *Cool colour scheme, with colourwashed tongue-and-groove walls*
3 *Pale tiled floor*
4 *Unfussy window treatments*
5 *Uncluttered lines to the sanitary-ware*
6 *Wooden accessories*

Opposite: An almost Gustavian-style basin, coupled with blonde wood, and subtly understated, patterned walls, give an air of quiet sophistication.

into a perfect bathroom just by repainting the walls and hanging new curtains. While redecoration will, of course, help to create the look you want, it is so much better when designing a new-style bathroom if you can allow a bit more budget to move any piece of sanitary-ware that is badly positioned. In a Scandinavian-style bathroom the fitments should be white or pale, with fairly classic, clean lines. If you have a pink floral suite, creating a Nordic look will be hard!

The best situation is to be starting completely from scratch; perhaps you are in the lucky position of converting an existing bedroom into a brand new bathroom, or building a new en-suite bathroom. Consult a professional bathroom designer if you are unsure about your ability to design an efficient bathroom, and really utilize the space properly. Consult him or her, too, about the wide range of available sanitary-ware with clean lines and pale colours, to help you decide on a new bathroom suite. If you find white a little too stark, you could choose cream or ivory, or even pale green or blue, without compromising the Nordic feel. Now, creating your Scandinavian-style bathroom will be much easier.

WALLS

Bathroom walls should be pale, perhaps with a very subtle pattern or texture which will add interest, but not draw attention, to the walls. You could choose one of the many wallpapers with understated, all-over patterns, although paper is not the ideal wallcovering in a bathroom with its steamy atmosphere. Alternatively, you could try a paint effect on the walls or ceiling, as you can give that a hard-wearing and water-resistant finish with polyurethane varnish.

A bathroom is usually fairly small, so it can be a good room in which to try something more difficult than colourwashing. Tongue-and-groove boarding is attractive and practical in a bathroom. You could use that on the wall as high as the bath splashback, and continue it around all the walls; above that you could apply a softly patterned wallpaper. Alternatively, you could line the bathroom entirely in tongue-and-groove, or old planks, and seal them with

The mellow tones of wood on the walls turn this bathroom into a snug, sauna-like room.

honey-coloured varnish to provide a wonderful warm cocoon of a bathroom reminiscent of a sauna.

FLOOR

Typical Scandinavian flooring in a bathroom would, of course, be sanded floorboards. But, a rather more practical idea in a bathroom is to use white or pale ceramic tiles. They would impart a clean and uncluttered look, and would provide a surface that is very easy to keep clean. Using tiles with a slightly raised texture would make the floor safer, as you would be less likely to slip.

WINDOWS

Bathroom windows are generally small so, for a Scandinavian look, simple dressing is important. Obviously, in a bathroom you need privacy so, even with frosted glass in the pane, some form of fabric is necessary to cover the window at night. A blind is practical, as you do not need to touch the fabric when pulling it, and there are many different versions; an Austrian blind, for example, can be very attractive (see page 74). Siting a mirror opposite or beside a bathroom window will apparently double its size and the whole bathroom will seem bigger on reflection.

LIGHTING

In a bathroom, the lights must either be operated by a switch outside the room, or by a string-pull inside, or be specifically designed for bathroom use with a sealed unit for safety. The lighting should be practical but not over-bright. You could have gentle wall lights to create a soft ambience for leisurely baths, and have a more focused light over the mirror and washbasin. The light will be enhanced if it is reflected in a large mirror. It would be sensible to install an efficient light to see to shave properly – too dim a light could be quite dangerous! Applying make-up and brushing hair is also much easier by a clear light.

ACCESSORIES

As in any Nordic-style room, the accessories in the bathroom should be made from natural materials, and in non-artificial colours, such as soft pastels or natural shades. Shelves and cupboards are vital for storage – look out in junk shops for sturdy wooden shelves that you could strip and colourwash. Towels can then be folded neatly and arranged in decorative piles. A thick, soft towelling bathmat, perhaps matching the shade of the tiles, looks great, and adds a pleasant feeling of luxury. Alternatively, you could make a rather more spartan, but no less authentic, Nordic bathmat out of wood (see page 72).

The large mirror situated beside the window doubles the daylight in – and the apparent size of – this bathroom.

WOODEN BATHMAT

A mat made of wooden slats, such as the one illustrated on page 66, gives a bathroom a clean-cut, austerely Nordic look. It is not difficult to make, and it would also be useful as a doormat in a hall or kitchen.

You will need

❋

- 315cm (12ft) best quality pine, 18 x 44mm ($\frac{3}{4}$ x 2$\frac{3}{4}$in) finished size
- 91.5cm (3ft) best quality pine, 18 x 28mm ($\frac{3}{4}$ x 1$\frac{1}{16}$in) finished size
- Metal tape measure
- Pencil
- Wood saw
- Coarse- and fine-grade sandpaper

- Drill with 6mm ($\frac{1}{4}$in) bit, 3mm ($\frac{1}{8}$in) bit and countersink bit
- Waterproof wood glue
- Cloth
- 24 screws, 38 x 8mm ($\frac{3}{4}$ x $\frac{5}{8}$in)
- Screwdriver
- Waterproof sealant or paint
- Paintbrush

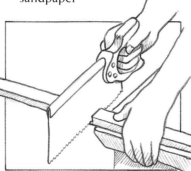

1 *Measure and mark the long length of pine into 60cm (2ft) lengths, and saw them up. Measure and mark the shorter length of pine into two 46cm (18in) lengths; saw it up precisely. Sand every side of each piece of wood with he coarse-grade sandpaper, rubbing all the edges and corners smooth to eliminate splinters. Then rub all over with the fine sandpaper for a final sleek finish.*

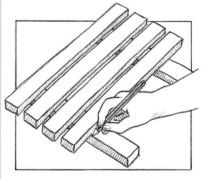

2 *Place the two shorter pieces of wood on a flat surface 51cm (20in) apart, and lay the top pieces centrally across them at intervals of 2cm (¾in), making sure that the top pieces are at right angles to the bottom pieces.*

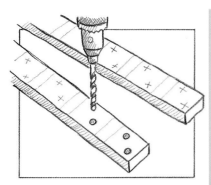

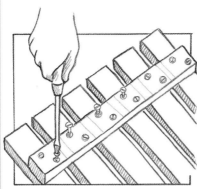

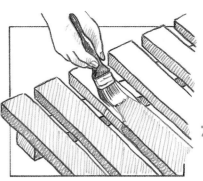

3 Mark the position of the top pieces on the bottom pieces using a pencil and ruler. Remove the top pieces and, in each resulting square on the bottom pieces, mark two screw holes diagonally opposite each other; you should have 12 on each base. Carefully drill these screw holes completely through the wood.

5 Drill a pilot hole for each screw through the existing screw holes, and insert the screws in their holes; tighten them up with the screwdriver. Ensure that the heads are sufficiently countersunk not to scrape the floor.

6 If you would like to apply some colour to the mat, now is the time. If not, give the whole mat, including the underside, a coat or two of a waterproof sealant such as matt yacht varnish. Leave to dry completely. Then enjoy your bath, knowing that you will never slip when you get out!

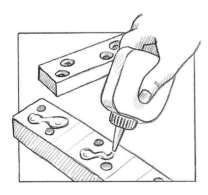

4 Fit the countersink bit to the drill and sink the screwholes on the underside of the base pieces. Apply glue to the base positions of each top section; stick all the pieces together in their correct order, removing any excess glue immediately with a damp cloth. Leave to dry.

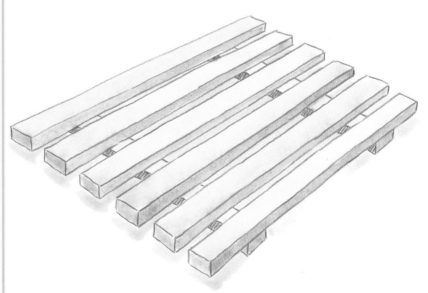

TIE-UP BLIND

This easy variation of an Austrian blind gives a more casual look to the window and is ideal for a small window, such as one in a bathroom. It would also be practical for a kitchen window, adding interest without interfering with worktops. It is not suitable for a window wider than 90cm (3ft), unless you add another tie in the centre.

You will need

- Tape measure
- Scissors
- Main fabric
- Border and tie fabric
- Pins
- Sewing machine
- Needle and matching thread
- Touch-and-close tape
- Wooden batten
- 2 or 3 x 5cm (2in) screws
- Screwdriver
- Fabric glue

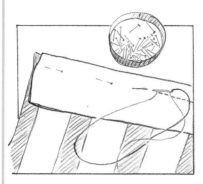

2 From your border fabric, cut three strips 11cm (4¼in) wide, which includes 5cm (2in) for turnings. Two strips should be the length of the blind fabric, the other the width of it, with 5cm (2in) extra for turnings. Lay a long strip along the edge of the blind with the right sides and edges of the fabric together; pin in position. Sew in place with a 2.5cm (1in) seam.

1 Decide whether you want your blind to hang inside or outside the window recess, and measure that, adding on 2.5cm (1in) to the length for a turning at the top. This is the size of the fabric for the blind, as the edges will be bound. Cut a piece this size from your main fabric.

3 On the other side of the strip, fold in a 2.5cm (1in) turning, wrong sides together and iron it in place. Fold the strip right over the raw edges of the blind, to the wrong side of the blind; pin and slip stitch in place by hand. Repeat with the other two raw edges of the blind, leaving the corners loose.

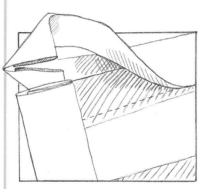

4 Take one corner and cut off the excess length of border along one long side. On the short side, fold in two corners of the border to the centre to form a mitre. Position it precisely to sandwich the raw end of the base of the blind; pin and hand sew in place. Repeat with the other corner.

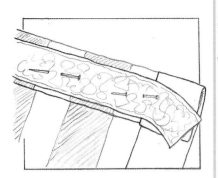

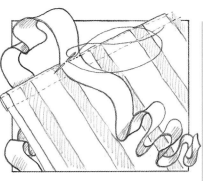

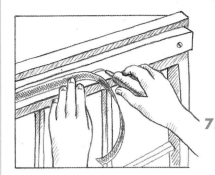

5 Fold in a turning of 2.5cm (1in) at the top edge of the blind. On the wrong side, and over the turning, pin the soft half of the touch-and-close tape. Machine stitch along both edges of this, taking care to make the seams as straight as possible since they will be clearly visible from the right side.

7 Sew two ties to the top of the blind, at the same point front and back, at about 15cm (6in) in from one edge. Repeat at an equal distance from the other edge with the two remaining ties. Now fix a batten across the top of the window using two or three screws, depending on its width.

8 Glue the rough side of the touch-and-close tape to the batten. When dry, press both sections of the tape together to fix the blind in position. Now gather up the blind to the height you want and tie the front and back ties together to hold it there.

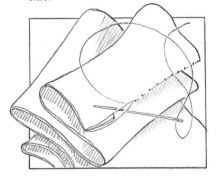

6 Carefully iron the finished blind. For the ties, cut four strips of border fabric the length of the blind and 10cm (4in) wide. Fold each one in half, right sides facing, and sew together down the long edge with a 12mm (½in) seam. Turn right side out and oversew the raw edges. Repeat with the other three ties, and iron them all.

CHAPTER EIGHT

ℒOFTS

SCANDINAVIA IS NORTHERN AND MOUNTAINOUS. Houses in such lands tend to have steeply pitched roofs to allow the snows of winter to fall off easily, keeping the inhabitants snug until spring. Rural Scandinavia is sparsely populated so, ironically, space is not at the premium that it is for those who live in kinder climates, and there is no need to look to the roof space for extra room at home. In more crowded conditions, more living space is always needed. So, have a look at your loft; it can be feasible to gain more space from the place you live in already, if it has a pitched roof. That unused loft could be very useful; you can create another room, or perhaps even more than one, if the roof is at a sufficiently pitched angle. Using your loft would be much less expensive than moving house!

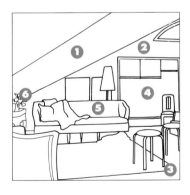

1 *Sloping roof of painted planks*
2 *White colour scheme to maximize light*
3 *Wooden floor, with brightly-coloured rug*
4 *Big window and simple blinds*
5 *Gustavian-style daybed with fresh checked cover*
6 *Attic space utilized well, with table tucked under eaves*

Exposed wooden beams form a stylish part of the decoration scheme, contrasting with the pale walls and adding character to this attic conversion.

ATTIC CONVERSION

A loft extension is excellent for any number of purposes. It can provide more bedrooms, an extra sitting room, a study, a workroom, a bedsit or a flatlet for older children, or whatever you need it to be. If you are going to be able to make a large light-filled room with wonderful views over surrounding countryside, it might be worth making the new room your main sitting room and turning the existing living room into a bedroom.

In order to make usable living space in your attic, ensure that your roof space is of a sufficient height – the finished room would need to be a minimum of 2.1m (7ft) high. You can increase some of the ceiling height by building on a large dormer window, if your neighbourhood council or similar authority will allow this. The ceiling joists need to be strong enough to form the basis for a new floor, and the struts and ties supporting the roof must be sufficiently well spaced not to impede the room available for your new accommodation. Another point requiring consideration is how to gain access from inside the house to your new space. A fixed staircase is usually necessary, whether it is a ready-made spiral staircase or a wooden version with ordinary treads and risers and a landing at each end. It depends on the space you have. If you are thinking of converting your attic, it is better to consult a professional loft extension firm first; they can tell you about the rules and regulations for your area, and whether your house will be able to bear the extra weight and so on.

Assuming all is well and you have built more accommodation in your loft, now you can think of decorating it.

WALLS AND CEILING

A room in the attic will need careful insulation if it is not to be very cold in winter and stifling in summer. Lining the whole room in timber planks looks wonderful, and the insulating qualities of wood would really come into their own here. If the planks are fitted well, they would accentuate beautifully all the interesting angles of the ceiling, as well as giving an attractive Nordic feel.

If the struts and ties of the roof were left in position, perhaps the roof beams could be exposed too. In this case, the rest of the walls should be painted white, and all the beams and supports stained to add to the resulting rustic character of the room. If there are no exposed beams, painting the walls white or a pale colour will provide a good basis for any room. You could then add a simple stencil to enhance the charm of all the angles, and give a little extra interest.

FLOOR

The floor in a Scandinavian-style loft needs no different treatment than a floor in any other part of a Scandinavian-style house, as outlined in this book. What you choose depends on the use of the

The interesting angles of an attic lend themselves to being accentuated by a decorative detail such as this stencilled ivy motif.

room. Look at the previous chapters for ideas. A children's playroom will need a smooth floor that is easy to sweep and keep clean; wooden planks would be good, as usual, as would cork with its natural warmth and softness.

WINDOWS

The windows in an attic are often difficult to curtain. The best and least cluttered solution for skylights is to leave them bare. Alternatively, they can be dressed with a simple cotton, unlined curtain, gathered top and bottom onto expandable wire, or even string as the peasants in their farmhouses used to do. The fabric is simply pulled to one side of the window during the day, then drawn across it at night (see page 82).

Dormer windows often have no room to draw curtains aside in the daytime. Here, a simple blind would work well – a roller, perhaps, or the tailored lines of a fabric roman blind.

LIGHTING

The type of lighting you choose depends on what purpose you are using your loft conversion for. Look at the preceding chapters for ideas. One point to remember is always to take care with candles and sloping ceilings; the flame can easily scorch the ceiling above it – or cause worse damage – if the flame has not got sufficient height to burn safely.

FURNITURE AND ACCESSORIES

What kind of furniture and accessories you choose for your attic will be determined by what you want to use the room for. But do not waste the space in the sloping eaves: build cupboards into the lowest angles, and install shelves to make a feature of slanting ceilings. A good piece of furniture for a Scandinavian-style second living room is a Gustavian daybed; the room can then have the dual purpose of acting as an extra guest room. If your loft has exposed beams, it would be a good location for Scandinavian folk-style chunky furniture and carpet runners.

Opposite: The sloping wooden wall and matching decor make this loft very inviting. The cupboard door is shaped to fit the eaves so that no storage area is wasted.

$\mathcal{P}$ROJECTS

SIMPLE STRUNG CURTAINS

Even the most inexperienced beginner can easily make these simple curtains. Hung on expanding curtain wire, they are useful for lofts as they can cover skylights or slanting attic windows with ease. It is not really a suitable treatment for a window wider than 90cm (3ft) or longer than 120cm (4ft). Choose a thin cotton or a sheer fabric – a fabric that is too thick cannot gather properly.

You will need

- Fabric
- Scissors
- Tape measure
- Iron
- Pins
- Sewing machine
- Matching thread

- Pencil
- Bradawl
- Screwhooks and eyes
- Expanding curtain wire
- Wire cutters
- Needle

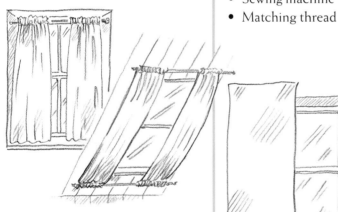

1 *Decide whether you are going to have the curtains strung across the top of the window frame or recess, with a simple hem at the bottom, or have them gathered on wire at both ends. These are then attached to the window itself, which is necessary on slanted windows for holding the curtains into the angle, or for windows that pivot to open.*

2 *Cut your fabric to size, making each curtain three-quarters the width of the window, plus 5cm (2in) for turnings. The length should be the depth of the window, plus 9cm (3½in) extra for turnings if you are having a gathered top and hemmed bottom, or 6cm (2¼in) for a gathered top and bottom; allow extra fabric for pattern matching if necessary.*

3 *On one side edge of a curtain, turn in a tiny hem (6mm/¼in); press it in position. Now turn that in again to form a hem of 12mm (½in); press, pin and sew in place. Repeat with all sides. If there is not a definite right side of the fabric, make sure that all the hems are facing the same way.*

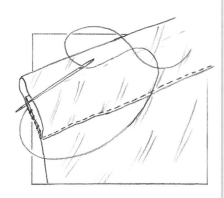

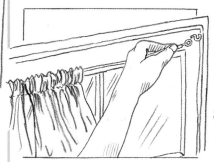

4 *On the top of one of the curtains, turn in a hem 1cm (½ in) and press it in position. Now turn that in again to form a casing of 2cm (¾in); press, pin and sew this in position, making as straight a seam as possible. Neaten the loose ends of the seams. Repeat with the top of the other curtain.*

6 *Stretch the wire tautly across the window and, using the wire cutters, cut the wire to fit precisely, remembering to allow for the extra length of the eye at the other end of the wire. Screw that eye into the newly-cut end of the wire, and feed it through the casing on both curtains. Hang the curtains up, ensuring that the wire hangs at tension; adjust if necessary.*

7 *Take down the curtains to finish the raw edges. If the bottom of the curtains are to be gathered as well, repeat steps 4 and 5 for both curtains and wire. If they are only to have a hem, turn in 1cm (½in) and press it; then make a hem of 5cm (2in), pin and sew by hand. Hang up your finished curtains!*

5 *Now mark the desired position of the top left side of the curtains with a pencil, and then pierce the point with the bradawl. Screw in a hook, and another at the same point on the right side of the window. Now screw a matching eye into the expanding curtain wire.*

CHAPTER NINE

SUMMER HOUSES

DURING THE 18TH CENTURY IT BECAME POPULAR to celebrate the long Scandinavian summers by leaving the towns and spending the summer season in a holiday home which was situated in the more healthy air of the seaside or the countryside. This custom was particularly common in Sweden and northern Denmark, where the coastline is more accessible than that of Norway and Finland. Indeed, the ruling classes of Sweden had been enjoying this summer pleasure since the Renaissance. But, eventually, the habit spread and summer houses for people of all walks of life sprang up all along the coastlines and neighbouring islands. Transport became easier, so that reaching an outlying island presented no difficulties. By the 1800s, enterprising builders had begun to erect houses for sale or rent on leased or freehold plots. Obviously some of the houses built

1 *Walls of horizontal painted planks*
2 *Unvarnished weathered floorboards*
3 *Curtains in unlined cotton*
4 *Old-style hurricane lamp*
5 *Re-covered director's chairs*
6 *Covering the bed with cushions turns it into a sofa by day*

Opposite: Here is an example of one-room living, summer house style. Every kind of activity is catered for; cooking, dining, reading, relaxing, and even sleeping. Note the particularly Scandinavian touches — the dried wreath, the wood and white interior, and the bright striped runners on the bare floorboards.

at this time were considered as important status symbols and much entertaining was done at the summer house; those houses were decorated and furnished as befits such style. Some superb examples can still be seen along the Stockholm archipelago today.

In the 1900s, the notion of escaping to the countryside in summer had become so popular that city councils started programmes, now called garden colonies, to let small garden plots, each with its own simple hut, to people who could not afford to get away from the cities.

20TH-CENTURY SUMMER HOUSES

Increased wealth during this century, especially after the Second World War, means that many people now have their own summer house, with the general exodus out of the towns becoming very marked at the height of summer. Having a holiday home – however tiny – is now almost considered no more a luxury than the family car. Simple cottages can be found all over Scandinavia. Tiny cabins are tucked into narrow Norwegian valleys or onto the edge of Norwegian shores, accessible only by boat; lakeside chalets nestle beside the northern forests; little beach huts lie beside the shores of many of the islands of the archipelago between Sweden and Finland; Denmark's flatter shoreline provides room for all kinds of holiday dwellings. Even cooler Iceland is not forgotten – tents are pitched for summer enjoyment and recuperation from the stresses of modern-day town life.

The ideal is to have a summer house within driving distance from the townhouse, so that families can use it as much as possible over the summer months. All the weekends can be enjoyed there - and perhaps even the odd midweek evening. Children can, of course, spend the whole summer at the summer house, although returning to town and school in the early autumn must be very stifling!

By their very nature, these homes are more casual and rustic than a full-time home (though there are some grander versions). Neglected barns and ancient fishermen's huts have been pressed into

use, and restored and rethought to form excellent summer homes. Usually all that is needed is just basic storage and rudimentary kitchen equipment, and somewhere reasonably comfortable to sleep. Folding chairs and tables are a must since meals are eaten outside, if at all possible, and all day is spent in the open air. So, weather permitting, the holiday home is most often in use during the evenings.

SUMMER HOUSE INTERIORS

Inside the summer house there is a sense of fun and relaxation. Colours chosen are often bolder, brighter and more summery than the more usual subtle tones – these look better in the stronger yellow light of the summer sun. A profusion of different cotton prints and patterns in cushions and pillows all blend exuberantly, adding to the carefree, holiday feel. Diverse styles of furniture are cheerfully mixed together. Sofas and armchairs of different shapes and sizes can be given a similar look by covering them with throws of matching or toning material; re-covering director's chairs in the same or coordinating fabrics will help the sense of continuity.

Space is usually at a premium in a holiday home. The living room will often need to provide room for a dining area and sometimes double up as a bedroom too. This is based on peasant living in, for example, the Finnish *tupa* or one-room cabin, where all family life went on in the one room. A flat sofa, rather than one with arms, can be used as a bed; if it is set against a wall, piles of cushions thrown onto it turn it into a perfectly comfortable sofa by day – and it looks good as well. Sometimes the kitchen is situated in a corner of this space, too.

Curtains should not be elaborate. Simple unlined cotton prints are probably best, or else sheer or lacy fabrics; these all look great when blowing softly in the warm breeze coming in at the open windows. Cotton rugs or rush mats are very practical; they are warm underfoot, but easy to shake outside when sweeping the floor to get rid of the sand, pine needles, or whatever else the family on holiday will bring in on their feet!

This little wooden summer house in a sunny garden is just the place for relaxing in the lazy sun-filled days of summer.

ACCESSORIES

Natural decorative ornaments look best in a rustic-style setting like a summer house. A herb or dried flower wreath is typically Scandinavian; hung on the wall, it will perfume the whole summer house, and it is very easy to make (see page 90). Other decorations can be dictated by the location of your holiday home. If it is a seaside cottage, pretty shells or starfish would make perfect ornaments; you could make pictures, mirror frames or decorative boxes with shells if the weather turns unkind. Or, if the house is tucked into a forest, pine cones or armfuls of foliage are ideal. For a lakeside holiday, what about using polished pebbles, or pieces of weathered driftwood as embellishments?

If you do not own a summer house, you could let your imagination run riot and create the atmosphere of a rustic Scandinavian summer house in one of the rooms in your home. Perhaps there is a little corner in the garden where you could build a summer house to dream in on sunny days.

DRIED HERB WREATH

A wreath of fragrant dried herbs or flowers is easy to make. An excellent place to hang it is the hall, as there is a welcoming scent as soon as you open the front door; the kitchen is also a good place, especially for a herb wreath, as the perfume of the herbs scents the air. But, wherever you hang it, a wreath will always remind you of the summer when you made it. You could base it on a ready-made dry-foam ring, but for a better result make your own base.

You will need

❋

- Circular wire ring, 20cm (8in) in diameter
- Reel of thin hemp string
- Sphagnum moss
- Scissors
- Dried aromatic herbs, such as rosemary, hops or bay leaves; or perfumed flowers
- Fine and medium florist's wires
- Gutta percha tape (available from florists)

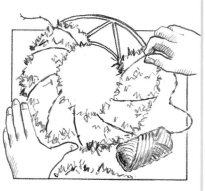

1 *First prepare the basic wreath. Take the wire ring and tie the end of the reel of string to it, leaving a short length beyond the knot. Put a generous handful of moss on the frame and start to bind it firmly in place by winding the string around and around the moss and frame. The moss should be should be about 2.5cm (1in) thick all around.*

2 *Add further handfuls of moss, overlapping one clump with another and binding firmly with the string as you go. Keep checking that the thickness of the moss is even. When you reach the starting point, overlap with moss, bind firmly, and find the loose end of the original knot.*

3 *Cut your binding string and tie the two ends together firmly. Leave to dry out thoroughly for about a week. Decide what kind of wreath you want – herbs, flowers or a combination of the two. Keeping to a single species will create a simple elegant wreath, while choosing lots of ingredients has a more complex and busy result.*

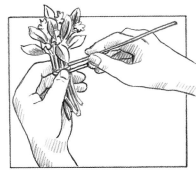

4 Now, wire items ready for inserting into the wreath base. For flowers, push a fine wire right through a single flowerhead and bend it above the bloom. Pull this hook back through into the flower, and twist the two ends together. For leaves, thread wire through the main vein, then bend the wire backwards behind the leaf and twist it together at the stem.

6 Do the same for small sprigs of three or four stalks. Arrange them as you like, and hold the stalks together in one hand, along with one end of a piece of medium wire. With the other hand, bend the wire behind and around the bunch, then twist it tightly around the stalks. Hide the wire by winding on gutta percha tape as before. Again, prepare lots of sprigs before you start arranging.

7 Take the dry base and insert wired sprigs at intervals around it, pushing the wire through the moss and bending the wires back into it. Continue inserting wired material around the moss wreath, adding more until you are happy with the effect. You may need to wire up more sprigs and leaves.

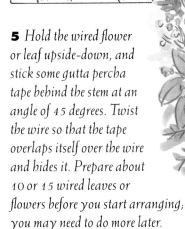

5 Hold the wired flower or leaf upside-down, and stick some gutta percha tape behind the stem at an angle of 45 degrees. Twist the wire so that the tape overlaps itself over the wire and hides it. Prepare about 10 or 15 wired leaves or flowers before you start arranging; you may need to do more later.

8 Twist together two medium wires to form a hanging hook. Decide where the hanging point will be and, at the back of the wreath, insert one end of the hook, twisting the wires securely into the wreath. Leave a fairly shallow loop, so that it will not be visible when the wreath is hung up, and secure the other end. Now hang your wreath wherever you wish!

RE-COVERED DIRECTOR'S CHAIR

Folding chairs are always useful when there are extra guests, especially in a holiday situation. As long as the frame of the chair is sturdy and in reasonable condition, re-covering it in new up-to-date fabric will give it a new lease of life.

You will need
❋

- Old director's chair
- Sharp craft knife
- Hammer
- Nail punch
- Fine-grade sandpaper
- Paintbrush
- Sealant or paint
- Strong fabric, such as canvas or closely-woven cotton
- Tape measure
- Scissors
- Pins
- Strong thread
- Sewing machine
- Tacks or staple gun and staples
- Iron

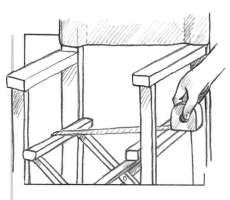

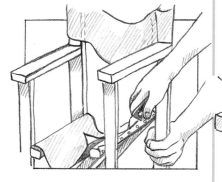

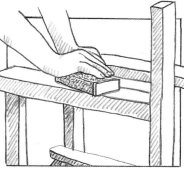

1 *Using a sharp knife, cut off the worn cover on the director's chair along both seat edges. Cut the old fabric away from any nails – do not try to prise them out of the frame as you might split the wood. Hammer old nails below the surface with the nail punch if you can; if they are round-headed nails, just leave them – the new cover will hide them.*

2 *If you want to prolong the life of the chair, sand down the frame well, and seal or paint it. It would lend itself well to being painted with a vibrant new colour. Leave to dry thoroughly.*

3 *Use the old cover as a pattern for your new fabric, if you can. If this is not possible, open out the chair and measure the distance between the outside edge of one of the rails, across the seat to the outside of the other edge; add 10cm (4in) to the length for turnings. Measure the depth of the old seat and add 8cm (3¼in). Cut out a piece of fabric this size.*

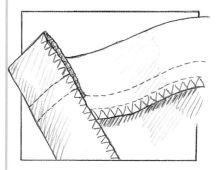

4 *Zigzag stitch along the front and back edges of the seat piece, to strengthen them. Turn over a hem of 4cm (1½in) at the back, over the zigzag, and press and pin in position. Use two rows of machine stitching, about 5mm (¼in) apart. Repeat with the front edge. Zigzag stitch both side edges, and fold in 3cm (1¼in) at each end; press it to hold the crease.*

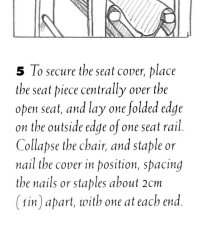

5 To secure the seat cover, place the seat piece centrally over the open seat, and lay one folded edge on the outside edge of one seat rail. Collapse the chair, and staple or nail the cover in position, spacing the nails or staples about 2cm (1in) apart, with one at each end.

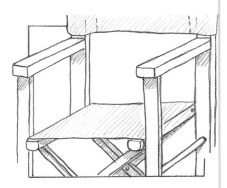

6 Repeat at the other side, starting by positioning one nail or staple at each corner. Open out the frame and check that the seat is not sagging; if it is, remove the two nails, take up the slack and re-staple. Hammer or staple securely all along the rail.

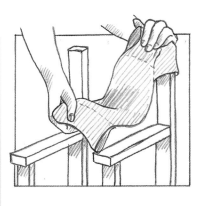

7 For the back piece, slide the old cover off both uprights and measure it, adding 8cm (3¼in) to the depth, and 3cm (1¼in) plus enough fabric for the casings for the uprights. Cut out a piece of fabric this size.

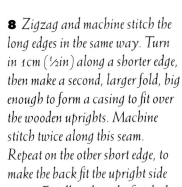

8 Zigzag and machine stitch the long edges in the same way. Turn in 1cm (½in) along a shorter edge, then make a second, larger fold, big enough to form a casing to fit over the wooden uprights. Machine stitch twice along this seam. Repeat on the other short edge, to make the back fit the upright side struts. Finally, place the finished back section back into position on the struts.

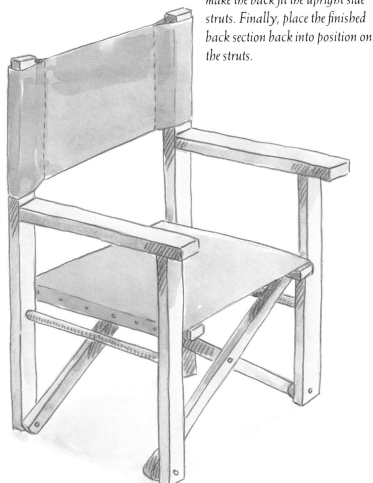

INDEX

ACKNOWLEDGEMENTS

Photographs courtesy of:

Pierced card lampshade from Acres Farm: 01734 744305 p.44; The Belvedere Gazebo from Amdega Conservatories: 0800 591523 p.89; Richard Bryant/Arcaid p.11; Laura Ashley p.60,84–5; Camera Press/Appeltofft p.87; Camera Press/Appeltofft/Appelgren p.78; *At Home: A Design for Living*, © Colour Library Books Ltd pp.20, 22, 71; from the Naturals Collection by Dulux: 01753 550555 p.13; from the Gentle Touch Collection by Dulux p.16–17; Anna French Ltd: 0171 351 1126 p.15; Jan Baldwin/Homes & Gardens/Robert Harding Syndication pp.48–9; Chris Drake/Country Homes & Interiors/Robert Harding Syndication p.7; Houses & Interiors pp.19, 39; Hülsta UK: 0171 629 4881 pp.40–1; Ikea Ltd pp.30, 36–7, 42, 76–7; Kingshill Designs pp.58–9; John Lewis Partnership p.63; Folklore Collection by Monkwell Ltd: 01202 762456 p.12; Trevor Moore: 01635 523990 p.52; Perstorp Flooring pp.10, 53; Sanderson: 0171 584 3344 pp.26–7, 29; Smallbone of Devizes: 0171 589 5998 pp.51,53; The Stencil Store: 01923 285577 pp.70, 79; Ulferts of Sweden Ltd: 01932 224979 p.9; The Velux Company: 01592 772211 p.80; The Water Monopoly: 0171 624 2636 p.69; Wicanders floor covering: 01403 710001 p.14; Wickes Building Supplies: 0181 863 5696 pp.66–7.